French Provincial Furniture

French Provincial Furniture

Robin
Ruddy

4880 Lower Valley Road, Atglen, PA 19310 USA

Library of Congress Cataloging-in-Publication Data

Ruddy, Robin.
    French provincial furniture/Robin Ruddy.
        p. cm.
    Includes bibliographical references and index.
    ISBN 0-7643-0205-1 (hardcover)
    1. Country furniture--France. I. Title.
    NK2548.R88   1998
    749.24--dc21   97-38783
                              CIP

Designed by "Sue"

ISBN: 0-7643-0205-1
Printed in China
1 2 3 4

Frontispiece photo:
Decorated in blue with glazed upper doors, this attractive escritoire was made in Provence around 1820. The rushed elbow chair in fruitwood dates also from 1820 and is from Provence, too. *Courtesy of L'Encoignure, London.*
Escritoire $6400-9600, chair $2500-4000 a pair

Published by Schiffer Publishing Ltd.
4880 Lower Valley Road
Atglen, PA 19310
Phone: (610) 593-1777; Fax: (610) 593-2002
E-mail: Schifferbk@aol.com
Please write for a free catalog.
This book may be purchased from the publisher.
Please include $3.95 for shipping.

Please try your bookstore first.

We are interested in hearing from authors
with book ideas on related subjects.

Acknowledgements

My sincere thanks to all those who gave me advice, information and permission to take photographs, often at the most inconvenient moments. In particular, Priscilla Chester-Master of Gloucester House Antiques, Isobel Simpson of L'Encoignure, Graham Arkcoll, Chris and Jo Harvey-Jones, Jill Palmer, Christopher Wilson, Shirley Rumsey, Linda Aiken, Adela Thomas, Dudley Hume, and Mario Walker of Mario Walker Restorations. And my special thanks to my wife, Paula, for her invaluable support throughout.

Please note: The value ranges that appear here are derived from compiled sources and were not supplied by the people acknowledged in the credit lines. The ranges were conscientiously determined to reflect the market at the time this work was compiled. No responsibility for their future accuracy is accepted by the author, the publisher, or the people credited with the photographs.

Picardy
and
Flanders

Normandy

Ardennes
and
Champagne

Brittany

Loire Valley

Alsace
and
Lorraine

Ile
De
France

FRANCE showing the
furniture regions

Burgundy, Bresse,
and
Franche-Comté

Poitou, Vendée,
and
Saitonge

Avergne

Lyons, Dauphine,
and
Savoy

Basque
and
Béarn

Languedoc
and
Roussillon

Provence

Contents

Introduction 9

Chapter 1. Competing Historical Influences: Louis XV Wins 15

Chapter 2. Woods of the French Countryside 23

Chapter 3. The Workshop of a Traditional Country Carpenter 28

Chapter 4. A Typical Country Home in the Nineteenth Century 34

Chapter 5. Furniture Styles of the Provincial Regions 37

    Normandy 38

    Brittany 55

    Loire Valley 61

    Poitou, Vendée, and Saintonge 64

    Basque and Béarn 79

    Languedoc and Roussillon 82

    Auvergne 85

    Provence 87

    Lyons, Dauphiné, and Savoy 95

    Burgundy, Bresse, and Franche-Comté 99

    Alsace and Lorraine 111

    Ardennes and Champagne 114

    Picardy and Flanders 118

    Ile-de-France 121

Glossary 126

Bibliography 127

Index 128

A fruitwood châpeau de gendarme armoire from Rennes. Also in fuitwood, but from Toulouse, is the early Languedoc commode dating from around 1760. The walnut table was made in the early eighteenth century in the Ile de France. *Courtesy of L'Encoignure, London.* Armoire $4800-8000, commode $16000-19000, table $3200-6400

Introduction

The Buffet of Monsieur and Madame Duclos

In your imagination, transport youself back to the year of 1847. The month is July, the place is Provence and the weather, as so often it is at this time of the summer, is searingly hot but tempered by a gentle, brow-cooling breeze.

By nine o'clock in the morning, Françoise Duclos has nearly finished her housework in the pink-washed home she shares with her husband Jean-Pierre and their four children. Outside, their home is typically Provençal, with turquoise blue shuttered doors, windows bordered in white, and dusty old red canal tiles on the roof, all surrounded by a green and aromatic garden of fruit trees, flowers and herbs.

Inside, the beamed rooms are furnished simply and practically with pieces which look almost part of the structure of the interior. Decoration is provided mainly by objects of everyday use: colorful plates, pottery and kitchen implements.

In the large kitchen, which also serves as a living room, Françoise is busy polishing a two-door fruitwood buffet which was made for them recently by a local craftsman using wood from trees on their own land. Its soft warm tones blend perfectly with the pinky yellow tiles of the floor and the brilliant sunlight shafting through the windows is both caught and deflected by the juxtaposition of straight and curved lines on the deeply carved surfaces of the

A two-drawer fruitwood and walnut buffet which is a near relative of the one in Madame Duclos' home. This one has more ornamental metalwork and vigorously carved escargot-style feet. $4000-5600

An oak armoire from Normandy shows the richness of design and carving that epitomizes the various similarities between work from the northern province and its southern counterpart, Provence. *Courtesy of Gloucester House Antiques.* $8000-9600

Right: The fruitwood armchair is nineteenth century but the upholstery is new. *Courtesy of Palmer Antiques.* $1600-2400

doors. A single drawer with sinuous moldings and a cut steel button handle sits over the doors of the buffet and a scalloped and highly decorated apron balances the overall design between galbé feet on sabots.

The style is at the same time rustic and sophisticated. The materials and finish show it to be a piece of country furniture for everyday use; sturdy and functional. Yet the confident carving and construction indicate that it has been made by an experienced and creative craftsman. If you can pinpoint a stylistic influence it is that of the Louis XV era, a good one hundred years earlier. But to Françoise it is as fashionable a piece of furniture as anyone would need.

She is probably not even aware that in Paris, many hundreds of kilometres away, the leading ébénistes of the period are favouring clean cut dark mahogany looks in a style known as Louis-Philippe.

In the country, the provincial artisans continue to work in their own fashion because they know that the furniture they produce is in harmony not only with the desires of their customers like Françoise, but also, and most importantly, with the shades and shapes of the rooms they are destined for.

Walnut chairs with multi-colored rushing are the traditional mainstays of old homes throughout France. *Courtesy of Gloucester House Antiques.* $800-900

An oak buffet à deux corps with simple steel trimmings and a prominent cornice, this example from Brittany follows stylistically the earliest type of storage cupboard. 88" x 64". $1920-2880

Now let us move forward more than one hundred years to the late twentieth century and visit again the same Provençal home in which Françoise and Jean-Pierre brought up their family.

Today the house is occupied by Alain Duclos, his wife Celeste, and their baby daughter. Alain is a direct descendant and the seventh Duclos to live in the property.

The changes are instantly obvious but on a second look are surprisingly cosmetic. There is a mailbox at the gate by the main road, a smart new Renault parked on the gravelled drive, an abundance of furnishing fabrics in rich Provençal colors throughout the home, pictures on the walls, a new cooker and chrome fittings in the kitchen, a large television set in the living room and a Minitel screen beside the telephone.

Françoise's pride and joy, the fruitwood buffet, stands in the same place still, catching the strong morning light as it has done for a century. Slightly darker now and showing some marks over its surface, its age is also revealed by the ravages of woodworm and winter damp, particularly on the back stile feet. Decades of careful polishing have given it the kind of sheen and patina which could be achieved in no other way. Only the passage of time could produce so much depth in a light colored wood.

Elsewhere in the house other pieces of furniture also remain unchanged. Mostly made in fruitwood, they include three armoires, a buffet à deux corps, a vaisselier, an horloge, a pétrin, several tables and numerous rush seated chairs in different styles.

My thanks to the Duclos family for allowing me to use them as an example. They are typical of many French provincial families in their recognition of traditional values and their desire to cherish what they believe to be of real quality and value. Unlike many families in other European countries, they did not cast out most of their old furniture in the (nineteen) sixties and seventies in favour of Formica. Inheritance laws also helped keep family furniture in place, and the result is that the best of French provincial furniture can still be found where it started out, in private homes throughout the land.

Fortunately for lovers of provincial furniture, the French have not kept it all for themselves. It is possible to buy a wide range of pieces in antique shops and markets, not only in France but also in the many countries to which they have found their ways over the years.

But how do you recognise a good piece of French provincial furniture? What are the distinctive motifs and decorations which distinguish it and how is it constructed?

In writing this book I have set out to provide some answers to these questions and to produce a straightforward guide to the subject. More detailed and academic studies can be found, especially in the French language, and I have named these in the bibliography. My personal research took me to shops and fairs in France where I could examine and compare types of furniture at first hand and capture as many as possible on film.

What I wanted to identify in particular were the key differences between French provincial furniture and other types of French furniture.

Few countries in the world are as rich and diversified in cultural heritage as France. The fact that the country boasts more than four hundred different types of cheese testifies to the independence and creativity of the people in the land's varying regions. But equally significant is the age-old contrast in ways between the capital, Paris, and the provinces.

With a coastline washed by four seas (the Mediterranean, Atlantic Ocean, English Channel and North Sea), and eight countries along her borders (Italy, Germany, Luxembourg, Belgium, Spain, Monaco, Andorra and Switzerland), France's countryside has developed strong regional differences. But the greatest divergence has always been between the regions and Paris itself. Historically Paris has typified the urbane while the provinces have represented the rural, and although this has been changing in modern France, the contrast is still evident.

The clear distinction between city, or Paris-style, furniture and country furniture began to crystallise as Paris asserted its dominance over the rest of France prior to the seventeenth century. It was further accelerated when Louis XIV, the Sun King, determined to make his court a centre of excellence in the design and manufacture of luxury goods. France's other major cities enthusiasti-

An elegantly molded door, full-length hinge and nicely carved escargot feet; this small walnut buffet is from the Loire. $1500-2000

cally copied as closely as they could the lead being set by Paris, but the craftsmen of the countryside, perhaps more influenced by factors of cost and practicality, took their time, selected only the aspects of decoration and construction that appealed to them, and in so doing created their own look, a style which has regional variations but is none the less recognisable - from Brittanny to Provence - as French provincial.

The resulting furniture is unique in its close and mutual kinship to the land from which it comes. Whether it is a massive armoire or a small rush chair, it seems as much a product of France's rich soil as is the wood from which it is shaped. Garlanded with carvings of fruit, flowers and birds, it could almost have grown alongside the trees and hedgerows of the countryside.

Until the mid-nineteenth century such pieces were usually created by travelling artisans, who, for a short period of time, would set up their temporary homes with their customers. They worked to order but with a creativity and inventiveness that rendered each piece an individual work of art. The wood to be carved was carefully chosen and dried, most often being taken from the land of the customer. It was perhaps oak, walnut or chestnut which an ancestor had planted and which generations had watched grow. These origins are at the heart of a provincial piece's distinctive character, and explain the regional variations which so characterize traditional country furniture.

Conceived for a specific destination in the home, in response to the particular requirements of the customer and made by artisans using local materials in a regional style, these pieces were infinitely more varied than the furniture of the château or its bourgeois adaptations.

The diffusion through the provinces of the influential styles of the day, be it Louis XV or Henry IV was equally varied. Gothic ornamentation could still appear in the mid-eighteenth century, Henry IV still reigned occasionally in 1750 and Louis XV continued in his full splendour in 1830.

Increased sophistication over the years did nothing to prevent the eleborate almost naive combinations of animal, floral and geometric motifs found in Basque, Breton or Savoyard work.

It is exactly this variety of styles, diversity of form, multiplicity of materials and techniques, and infinite flexibility of ornamentation that makes regional furniture so attractive to the contemporary eye, and such a welcome change from the elements of functionalism in modern life.

An old armoire from Lower Normandy or a Provençal buffet can no longer be regarded as merely regional items produced on the margins of a sophisticated world. They are, on the contrary, perfect works of creation in their own right, irreducible to mundane stylistic standards or plastic uniformity.

They are works of destiny, each with a unique history, each imbued with the sap of the land and the touch of countless users over the decades. Our imagination runs with them; the perfume of lavender in an armoire, traces of flour in a pétrin, the aroma of cider in an old buffet, and the presence of previous generations with their old sayings, ways of life and forgotten dialects.

This innate and powerful sense of past explains why a good piece will bring something special to any surrounding, be it a traditional home like that of the Duclos family or an eclectically furnished modern apartment or house.

This book pays tribute to the felicitous combination of country wood, hand carving, warm patination, graceful styling and sheer character which gives French provincial furniture a unique and unsurpassed quality of its own.

Right: A perfect conversation seat for two; ideal for outdoor use in the South of France, where it was made in the nineteenth century. *Courtesy of Palmer Antiques.* $1600-2400

Chapter One
Competing Historical Influences: Louis XV Wins

Third to Fifteenth Centuries

Although sophisticated and beautiful furniture was produced in the ancient world by the Egyptians, Greeks and Romans as well as in the Orient, the aesthetic and technical advances which were made at that time were sadly lost in the ensuing Dark Ages of Europe.

Saber legs developed by the Greeks, carved animal feet from Egypt and motifs such as acanthus leaves, paterae (oval rosettes), egg and dart, and festoons of laurels or grapes were all forgotten until the Renaissance.

From the third to the fifteenth century furniture ceased to be a sought after commodity in France, as elsewhere. Instead, designers and craftspeople applied their talents primarily to architecture.

Information about furniture in France during the first 900 years A.D. is scarce and comes mainly from surviving literature and manuscript illustrations. It appears that quality became a consideration only on the few occasions when a strong regional ruler established a stable seat of government which permitted improvements to the general standard of living.

Geometric patterns typified decorative work of the early centuries, evoking strength and solidity.

In the Middle Ages the comparatively frugal way of life at all levels of society was reflected in the basic nature of the furniture. The meagre sleeping and eating facilities of a peasant's home were usually contructed literally as part of the building and not moveable in any way. Very often, the only mobile elements of a home were its coffers, pétrins, tables and seats. Everything else was conceived as part of the interior design. Reduced space meant that the walls were extensively utilised for hanging clothes and holding utensils for cooking, eating and daily life, that is, where the walls were strong enough.

In time, as the traditional single communal room gave way to a series of rooms, so the first popular mobile pieces of furniture began to appear, such as armoires, beds and buffets.

A significant innovation was the closed cupboard, created initially to hold food, The existing system at that time was a basic series of shelves left open to display drinking vessels and plates. The new version had doors, often featuring decorative open work or grilles to allow in the air.

Equally important was the arrival of the press, a cupboard in which clothes could be either hung or laid flat. These could be found at first in ecclesiastical foundations, but their popularity spread and they soon began to replace the traditional coffer as a storage unit. In England an enclosed cupboard of this type was called an aumbry or armoury, while in France it was termed an armoire.

Later in this period the Gothic style which had come to dominate the arts and architecture from the late twelfth century also influenced carpenters and joiners, who appropriated its ornate arcading, pinnacles and tracery.

But often the most important element of home furnishing was fabric in the form of wall hangings and curtains to keep out the draughts.

Left: Early furniture looked like part of a building and the armoire was intended to be functional rather than decorative. *Courtesy of Gloucester House Antiques.* $4000-5600

A buffet à deux corps was created to make maximum use of room height. The top section can be placed on the bottom half, then the cornice slid on to leave only inches or less between it and the ceiling. In some cases the cornice was done away with entirely. $2880-3840.

Proportions depended on the sizes of the individual homes. This walnut buffet à deux corps is taller than average at 95". *Courtesy of Gloucester House Antiques.* $4000-5600

Right: Elaborate patterns were a feature of wood carving up to and beyond the Renaissance period. This door in Lyons illustrates the kind of work found equally on furniture.

The front of this bookcase epitomizes the move away from the practical and towards the decorative that came about under Louis XV. $1600-4000

Renaissance

King François I of France (1515-1547) wrestled with his friend King Henry VIII of England and won the first and only fall. But his real claim to fame was as a patron of the arts.

Only a year after becoming king he persuaded the great Leonardo da Vinci to grace his court for three years. The curvaceous and exuberant styles of Italy were imported to France and their influence spread gradually to the provinces. It was at this time that walnut first came to be preferred to oak.

Louis XIII (1610-1643)

Although the main shapes of furniture changed little, there was a growth in the use of turned decoration for table and chair legs, stretchers and decorative work. Moldings became heavier and in provincial work often covered the main part of a buffet or cabinet. Geometric patterns were typical of the period as were heavy cornices and flattened bun feet. Upholstery and cushions started to take the place of hard seats in some parts.

Louis XIV (1643-1715)

If furniture can be said to reflect what is happening in society itself then the developments of the seventeenth century were a clear illustration of the divergence that was beginning to manifest itself between court and country.

Louis XIV, supported by his finance minister Colbert and a leading artist of the day, Charles Lebrun, conceived a major project destined to establish France's premier position as an exporter of luxury goods. Together they launched the Gobelin project, a grand enterprise based at a huge workshop near Paris, where master craftspeople produced elaborate rugs, fine laces, paintings, ornate silerware and splendid tapestries.

Lebrun became the first director of La Manufacture Royale des Meubles de la Couronne, with responsibility for the quality control of design and execution for all furnishings made for the court. In this way an overall style was ensured and the predominance in Paris of the designer over the craftsman was established. It was the historic first step in France's climb to pre-eminence as a source of luxury goods.

But it was all in direct contrast to the simple pattern of demand and supply which still existed in the provinces, where artisans continued to produce personalised pieces of furniture to meet their customers' particular needs, often without knowing exactly how they would turn out until the job was done.

In Paris there was to be no improvisation as techniques became ever more sophisticated. In the early eighteenth century André-Charles Boulle perfected a method of veneering furniture using combinations of tortoiseshell, ebony, pewter, brass and mother of pearl. His highly distinctive effects were at the opposite end of the spectrum to provincial work.

Baroque, from the Italian word *barroco* meaning a misshapen pearl, also made its debut, lavishly decorated with heavy carvings, figural sculpture and swooping shapes.

But still the furniture makers of the French provinces carried on in their own ways, stopping occasionally to appropriate a detail of style or shape for their own purposes.

Louis XV (1715-1774)

It was during the comparatively long reign of Louis XV that there appeared a new style that was to have universal appeal.

What regional manufacturers liked about the so-called Louis XV rococo style was the way it gave their furniture a lighter and more decorative appearance without reducing its physical strength or practicality.

A deviation of the French word *rocaille*, meaning fancy stonework for fountains, rococo was typified by a lighter and more fanciful look than the preceding baroque. Its repertory of shells, vases, fronds, figures, fruit and flowers, originally taken from the designs of Meissonier and Pineau, produced light and pleasing decorations on flat surfaces as well as three-dimensional effects, all of which translated effortlessly to the large expanses of an armoire or buffet.

In provincial France the decorative appeal of Louis XV merged happily with the solidity of a sturdy oak armoire like this. *Courtesy of Gloucester House Antiques.* $3200-4800

The evolution of regional furniture had progressed steadily from the heavy, cubic styles of the pre-Renaissance period with its thick planks, fat feet and geometric shapes. Now, with the arrival of Louis XV style, it was to accelerate to new heights of inspiration.

The typical armoire lost its small rectangular panels in favour of large, curvaceous sections often following complex and delicate outlines. Curves, counter curves and whirls constituted the essential decoration, while the base was transformed by turnings and carvings which ran smoothly into the fine camber of the feet. Thinner woods began to be used and colored stains brought fresh highlights to the ornamentation.

The decorative fantasies which were permitted by Louis XV style were to result in its continuing popularity throughout provincial France right up to the start of the twentieth century. Although slow to develop, the love affair with Louis XV proved both rewarding and enduring.

This was a key period in general for furniture development and before moving on it is worth noting that private homes in Paris began to be furnished more for comfort and elegance than for grandeur, resulting in the first appearance of smaller pieces, such as the writing table, the desk and the commode. All these, as well as the bergère, an armchair with caned or upholstered sides, and the marquise, a double armchair, were to reach the provinces before long.

Louis XVI (1774-1792)

Louis XVI style arrived in its time, and although not as influential as Louis XV style, brought new rectilinear lines with straight drawers, sharper edges and straight turned feet. Strong neoclassical elements came in largely as a result of the earlier appointment of the Marquis de Marigny, the brother of Madame de Pompadour, to a senior post in 1751. His visits to Italy marked the beginning of the court's interest in classical forms for furniture, and gave birth to what is known as the Transitional Period, the joining of Louis XV and Louis XVI styles in which the straight lines of neoclassicism and the curves of rococo are combined.

In terms of design influence on provincial furniture this was also an important period. During the nineteenth century such combinations were seen increasingly, and somehow the marriage of these theoretically disparate elements produced a truly distinctive flavour.

Directoire (1793-1799)

A more academic classicism was introduced in the post-Revolution period. It had limited influence outside Paris.

Empire (1799-1815)

Although their place in history cannot be diminished, the Emperor Napoleon and his Empress Josephine were, in their way, pioneers of theme decoration. They employed architects Percier and Fontaine to conceive a panoply of motifs to evoke an atmosphere of antique grandeur and a mood of absolute monarchy. Egyptian decorations, dark woods such as mahogany, brass handles and gilt bronze mounts were typical elements which did not appeal to those in the country. But they adapted some facets, such as stars, medallions, palmettes and oval paterae, which were usually carved in wood.

An Empire look for rustic chairs in cherry, on the left, and walnut. *Courtesy of Gloucester House Antiques.* $1200-1600

Restoration (1815-1830), Charles X (1824-1830), Louis-Philippe (1830-1848)

Each of these eras merits genuine appreciation for the elegant and understated lines they introduced, but they were to have minimal effect outside Paris.

Interestingly, it was this period, the first half of the nineteenth century, which was to see the richest and most felicitous examples of regional furniture emerge from the hands of the local craftsmen.

By carefully selecting elements of sophisticated city styles from the past and merging them with rural traditions they created furniture which was both classic and original. It was a veritable Golden Age for French provincial furniture.

The nineteenth century influences of the Restoration and Charles X periods were also reflected in country furniture like this walnut armoire. *Courtesy of Palmer Antiques.* $4800-6400

Chapter Two
The Woods of the French Countryside

Two distinct types were used to make French provincial furniture: the wood of fruit trees and the wood of forest trees.

While Parisian ébénistes were experimenting with exotic imported woods like amboyna, mahogany and kingwood, the people of the provinces were continuing to follow the philosophy of life that had sustained them so satisfactorily in the past - to use as materials what was readily at hand and what was sustainable.

They selected the woods literally on their doorsteps, and in so doing they unconsciously created a natural harmony between the finished furniture and its place of origin.

Their actual choice depended on the design they had in mind. For instance, oak, walnut and pear were found to lend themselves best to furniture with a rectilinear, architectural look. If the need was for cambered feet, curved shapes and crosspieces with turned profiles, then the preference was for fruitwood. That is why the best Louis XV inspired pieces are often in cherry or wild cherry.

Where more fantasy or color were demanded, as with Louis XV and XVI styles, so the choice might be for speckled panels, made from burr ash or elm.

The fruitwood frame of an armoire is complemented by panels in polished walnut. The grain of the walnut has turned black in places as it does usually in time. $4800-6400

A large part-glazed, three-door bookcase in fruitwood from Beaune, circa 1775. The writing table in merisier is from Normandy, circa 1790. The walnut desk chair is from the late nineteenth century. *Courtesy of L'Encoignure, London.* Bookcase $19,000-24,000, table $4500-6400, chair $1600-2400

Left: Mixing wood in a piece was done sometimes for decorative purposes and sometimes out of necessity. This armoire includes no less than five different woods. The panels are in walnut, the front framework in beech and the faux-dormant in oak. The cornice is in poplar and the sides in poplar and beech. $4800-6400

The light colored pearwood used in this buffet gives it a distinctive character but one which would undoubtedly have been in harmony with its original rural surroundings. *Courtesy of Palmer Antiques.* $4800-6400

In some regions, notably the Ile-de-France, Poitou, Saintonge, Touraine, Burgundy and the Lyonnais, the contrasting of different woods became especially popular, bringing with it appealing mixtures of color and texture. In a single piece, while rich cherry might be the choice for the frame, the panels could be in a lively ornamental burr wood.

Whatever the preference, the wood always came from the meadows, hedgerows or forests of the region.

The fruitwoods would be mainly cherry, wild cherry, pear, apple, lime or lemon. The forest woods: oak, walnut, chestnut, beech, ash, larch, elm or pine. But other woods were also used from time to time, such as mulberry, plum, birch, poplar and service. If certain species were more popular in particular areas it was probably as much to do with their abundance as anything else,

Oak was highly esteemed in Lower Britanny, for example, while, very occasionally, an exotic wood like mahogany might figure in a piece made close to a major sea port, such as Nantes. Sometimes the choice of wood depended on local traditions. In the Macon area, it is said, chestnut was regularly picked for a special quality - its reputed capacity to repel spiders.

Recognizing and appreciating woods can add immeasurably to your enjoyment of provincial furniture, but remember that even for an expert it is often difficult to identify a species, especially among the fruitwoods. Age, staining and polishing will all affect the appearance of a wood, providing a wonderful patination but hindering accurate identification.

The following is a list of some of the major woods and their distinctive qualities:

Cherry
A warm reddish colored wood used for solid construction in France mainly after 1750. Highly suited to carved work.

Lime
A soft, close grained wood of a creamy white color, darkening slightly to yellow. A favourite with carvers.

Pear
A strong, hard wood, not unlike lime, and varying in color from pink to yellowish white. Fine even grain and texture.

Apple
A rich, reddish brown in color, very hard and used for turned work or flat surfaces when large boards were available.

Oak
A hard pale yellow wood that darkens with age and polishes to a rich glowing brown. Clearly grained and widely used.

Walnut
Noted for its fine finish, walnut was used in France from the Renaissance period. Good for carving although susceptible to woodworm, it can confuse due to the range and variety of graining. The grain of polished walnut can look black.

Chestnut
A pale yellowish wood, sometimes tinged with pink. The grain is close and even but the wood is soft and not always durable.

Beech
Many French chair frames are in beech, either polished, painted or gilded. Fairly hard, with straight, fine, close graining ranging in color from pale to light reddish brown.

Ash
Unsuitable for carving, very vulnerable to woodworm but nevertheless popular for inexpensive country furniture. A tough, light brown wood. Ash burrs were suitable for decorative veneers.

Elm
Coarsely grained, somewhat similar to oak in appearance but softer and more susceptible to worm. Pale brown, sometimes with a reddish hue, it has a characteristic growth ring. Used for chairs and large boarded pieces.

Walnut, like cherry, found favor in all parts thanks to the fine finish it provided. And time proved that it got better with age. $3600-6400

Cherrywood was popular in most of France. Highly adaptable, firm but clean to work, and, of course, beautifully colored, it was used for everything from buffets, as here, to tables. $2400 - 3520.

Pine

Straight grained soft wood used mainly for carcasses. Often painted.

Larch

A hardish wood, strong and durable. Varying in color from reddish brown to pale yellow and used mainly for carcass work.

Right: Elm and oak were often used together, but when stains were used they could look much darker than this.

Chapter Three
The Workshop of a Traditional Country Carpenter

Surrounded by buttercups and the flowers of the meadow. As likely as not that was where the traditional craftsman set about creating an armoire or buffet for a customer. That was his workshop.

For the most authentic pieces were made on the spot, right next to the fermettes or maisons they were destined to complement. Good weather permitting, and in the South the climate was more often than not favourable for carpenters and joiners out of doors, the job would be done on site. A space was cleared, timber was selected from the customer's own land, each section was carefully chosen and honed, and the work commenced in a fashion that was both swift and careful, observed with great interest from time to time by the craftsman's appreciative clients, their children and members of the family who visited regularly.

The finished article, made exclusively for its new owners, was regarded with great pride, and in the decades which ensued, passed with respect from generation to generation; often oc-

The fruitwood top of a farmhouse table shows the broad planks which carpenters used. Pegs were made to pin them to the base, in this case made of oak. $1200-2400

The long central upright of this glazed oak armoire is faux dormant, and attached to the door on the left.

cupying the same special position in a particular room of the home.

Much furniture was made by travelling artisans who set up their outdoor workshops on site and worked to an overall design agreed with the customer. But a proportion was made by local carpenters operating from workshops in the communal living rooms of their own homes.

Usually a craftsman worked alone, though occasionally his son or an apprentice helped out. When the craftsman worked at a customer's home he was found a place to sleep and ate with the family.

An entire ritual would attach to many of the projects, as with the preparation or an armoire destined to be the dowry of a daughter of the house.

Several months before the wedding the armoire would be ordered. Even before the daughter's birth the trees for the necessary timber would have been selected and reserved, often with the intention of using mixed woods such as oak for the legs and fruitwood for the panels. The bride's parents would sit down with the carpenter to discuss styles and the latter would suggest several suitable models. These designs would be adapted to meet the particular requirements of the future owners, not least in terms of proportions, and only then would work commence.

Sometimes a simple ceremony took place to mark the felling of a tree which had been earmarked for a special piece.

The craftsman would on occasions carve a date on the front to record the setting up of the young couple's new home, or perhaps add the bride's initials. But very rarely would he sign his own work, and his creations would remain anonymous.

Attempts to identify individual craftsmen have nearly always met with failure, but occasionally it is possible to trace a particular maker by following a series of clues.

One such success was in the region of Sennecy-le-Grand, close to Chalon-sur-Saône in the South East, where a remarkable type of armoire can be found which is notable for its huge dimensions, hinges which stretch from top to bottom and single drawers in the base. Researchers were lucky to find an owner of such an armoire who knew that it had been made by his own great grandfather as a dowry for his daughter. The great grandfather was one Claude Laborier, who was born in 1819 and died in 1864, and further research showed that throughout his working life he had recreated the same distinctive style of furniture. From that point it was relatively easy to discover other examples in the region, to reconstruct his life and career and to build up a catalogue of his work.

But for every one recognized artisan, countless others must remain unknown.

What is certain, however, is that most joiners developed their own styles, patterns and types of construction and once they had established a successful format they tended to continue with it, subject only to variations in size, carving or ornamentation. Of course, some liked to experiment with new ideas and occasionally the first tentative steps in a new direction can be discerned in a piece.

Accumulated traditions lay behind the work of each craftsman. Old models would be referred to, tools passed from father to son would be used and so would established stencils and templates.

The craftsman's array of tools featured planes, chisels and saws, each with a specific purpose. Braces, mallets and measuring equipment, all with colorful and distinctive names, made up the wide selection.

Construction often involved tenon and mortice joints with sections secured by pegs rather than glue. Not only did pegging speed up the construction process, because there was no need to take apart a piece to glue it and no need to wait for glue to dry, it also allowed for movement in the finished piece during extremes of temperature in the era before central heating and air-conditioning. Since veneers were hardly ever used it was normal in the country for pegs and dovetails to be left clearly visible.

Local weavers also played their parts in the process. Here, an elm seat still has its original handwoven base in surprisingly good condition. Circa 1800.

Steel hinges like these were made throughout France with minor regional variations. Their pin and socket construction made it a simple job to remove doors from the carcass when necessary.

Practicality was also behind the development of the faux-dormant, a technique in which the central upright of the frame of an armoire or buffet was attached instead to one of the doors. When closed the piece looks as if it has two doors closing on an upright, which is often decorated. When you open the doors, one of them, usually the left, takes with it the strut, thus providing unimpeded access to the shelves and facilitating the laying out of flat linen. The door with the faux-dormant is commonly kept shut with a hook which attaches to the middle shelf.

Such a common-sense approach also led to the construction of some armoires in "kit form," with doors, sides and backs made to slot into each other so that the piece could be carried in sections along narrow corridors or up winding stairways. The cornice was usually also made separately for similar reasons. In these ways a large armoire could be installed in a room not much wider or taller than itself.

The quality of carving varied enormously since the specialization encouraged in the city was not available in the provinces. Some carpenters excelled at construction but were limited in their abilities as carvers, others were the reverse.

The amount of ornamentation on a piece also depended on how much the customer was able to pay. Better pieces were distinguished by the quality of their back boards, while less expensive items were given more primitive backs.

Natural local waxes would be used to finish a piece but the color of the timber would be allowed to show through. In time the pieces would gradually darken down, but, of course, those left in sunlight could well take on a lighter patina, not necessarily displeasing if evenly spread.

Metalwork is a significant feature of much provincial furniture, and is normally in iron, copper or brass. Hinges, knobs and keyhole surrounds, often highly elaborate in design, are the main metal items found on most pieces, and were commissioned from the local blacksmith or locksmith.

Another less attractive feature of much old furniture is woodworm. It must have been as unwelcome a presence in an eighteenth century home as it is today in modern surroundings, but a totally satisfactory solution for dealing with it has yet to be found.

For some reason French worm often appears to produce larger bore holes than its cousins in other countries. One theory is that fruitwood from the French countryside tastes better. Either way, a certain amount of *picure*, as some call it, does not spoil the appearance of a piece. Crumbly sections, though, require either professional filling or replacement, and skilled renovation has restored the beauty of much furniture that some would have considered beyond hope.

If you study closely any of the provincial pieces influenced by Parisian styles you will find that none is a direct equal in terms of construction and finish, but that, in effect, their real advantage is that they have what the French would call *"un aspect campagnard"*.

In their build, in the use of woods, in the techniques of assembly, in their choice of motifs and in the decorative finish they remain completely country style, with a form of naivety that distinguishes them totally from refined city pieces.

A curious detail, an innocence in execution, an error, perhaps, in overall proportion, a slip in scale, a rudimentary finish to the sides other than the front - all these elements provide a special charm and tell us that this is a genuine product of rural craftsmanship.

Decorative steel keyhole surrounds are the perfect visual partners to well-polished fruitwood. They were made to order by local blacksmiths or locksmiths. Later, copper or brass became popular.

Chapter Four
A Typical Country Home in the Nineteenth Century

The principal clients of artisans and joiners were historically as much the farmer and peasant as the well-to-do.

Even in the most modest farmhouse or fermette, it was not unusual just sixty years ago to see a selection of beautiful furniture lined up along the walls of the main communal room.

The russet color of a bed made of chestnut would catch the light next to the blonde haloes of the panels of an armoire in wild cherry. They bore witness to the daily life of a country family which was proud to have furniture made specially for it. A regional home with its own traditional furniture expressed continuity and respect for a life of work and rest spent together.

French researchers carried out a series of important surveys in the 1940s despite the difficulties imposed by war and occupation. Their aim was to visit traditional homes throughout the country and to record as much detail as possible about the furniture in them. They took photographs, listed dimensions and wrote down anecdotes recalled by the furniture's owners. Their findings are now in the French national archives and provide an invaluable picture of the past.

Their timing was crucial. Many of the interiors were exactly as they had been since the nineteenth century, and the researchers

Left: Well-used but sturdy fruitwood chair made for a more affluent country home. $400-600

Right: A walnut child's chair. $400-1200

Rush-seated chairs, such as this one from Poitou, were made in a wide range of designs and homes usually possessed a mixed collection. $560-800

Variations in the turning provided a more sophisticated appearance for some chairs. $560-800

A group of four fruitwood chairs (with some broken stretchers) pictured at a fair in the South. They are from the southern part of the Lyons region. $800-1280.

Like chairs, tables in provincial homes were given regular daily use. Solid construction, with stretchers for extra strength, was given precedence over design fashions. $1280-2800

were able to see pieces in situ and record information about when and how they were made. A few years after would have been too late. The arrival of electricity and water in rural communities resulted in numerous modernized homes with new kitchens, bathrooms and a consequent re-organisation of internal furnishings, although the actual pieces were usually kept.

Another valuable source of information is the archives of local notaries, whose duty it was to draw up inventories of contents in connection with marriage contracts or following the death of the master or mistress of a house.

One such archive describes the home and contents of a cooper from Clessé in the Saône-et-Loire, who died in 1863 leaving a widow and two young children.

The house consisted of two first floor rooms together with a kitchen and a small room with a sink in it, all reached by an interior staircase at the end of a short corridor. On the ground floor were a cellar, a barn, stables, a hay store and a shed.

Furniture on the upper floor consisted of plain beds made from walnut, a four-door buffet also in walnut, a long refectory style table and six chairs, all slightly different in style. Also in evidence were a small night table with a single drawer, a round table with five legs and a gilded mirror on the wall. Simple furnishings, but each item was lovingly preserved and cared for.

A more elaborate interior was described by researchers in the Haute-Saône. The communal room was reached by a small corridor from the front door. In it was a fireplace topped by a wooden mantel featuring a pair of hearts and a date, 1874. A pétrin with turned feet stood against a wall close to an oak armoire on bun feet and a vaisselier. A fine piece, this dresser showed the stylistic influences of both Louis XV and Louis XVI in its curved feet and shaped door panels, with a false front frame and three shelves with balustrades and fluting. What a find such a piece would be today.

Elsewhere in the main room were a beautifully carved grandfather clock, two medium sized fruitwood tables and four chairs. Simplicity was the keynote, not because money was short, but because every piece had a job to do. No piece was there purely for decorative purposes; but its color, form and ornamentation nevertheless made it a delight to the eye.

Chapter Five
Furniture Styles of the Provincial Regions

General de Gaulle once protested, "How can a man be expected to govern a country which produces more different types of cheese than there are days in the year?"

It was de Gaulle, incidentally, who chose a Normandy armoire as a gift for the Americam General Spiers following the Second World War. His taste in furniture was obviously as keen as his awareness of the regional complexities of this great country.

Sometimes it is the differences that you notice, sometimes the similarities. In the following sections I have therefore aimed to pinpoint the differing design and construction characteristics of each of fourteen separate regions in order to avoid needless repetition of their similarities.

Starting in Normandy, I have worked more or less anticlockwise round France to select the key elements of design in Brittany, the Val de Loire, Poitou and the Vendée, the Basque and Béarn, the Languedoc and Roussillon, the Auvergne, Provence, Lyons, the Dauphiné and the Savoy, Burgundy, Bresse and the Franche-Comté, Alsace and Lorraine, the Ardennes and Champagne, Picardy and Flanders, and, finally, the Ile de France.

This fruitwood table with sliding drawers is from the Vendée and is a near relative of the Breton table à glissants, circa 1735. The backdrop is an Aubusson tapestry of about 1700. The rare green confit pots are from the south-west. *Courtesy of L'Encoignure, London.* Table $4800-8000, tapestry 6400-9600, pots $190-240 each

Normandy

Gastronomically, Normandy is renowned for its apple and dairy products. Farm cider, Calvados apple brandy, and creamy cheeses like Livarot, Camembert and Pont l'Evêque are world famous.

The use of exposed wood in the region's timbered colombage buildings is equally renowned, and this skilled way with wood is as apparent in the region's furniture.

Furniture making began to flourish in the seventeenth century as the Normans' maritime commerce brought prosperity to the province. As in other parts of the country, most pieces were built at the customer's home, but the agriculturally rich towns of Fécamp, Yvetot and Caen became early centers of production.

Oak was normally the choice for the finest pieces, while pine, although softer and easier to carve, was reserved for humbler work. Elm, apple, beech and chestnut were also popular and mahogany, which Norman sailors brought back from the Caribbean, appeared occasionally in the late eighteenth century in towns near ports like Rouen.

The construction of colombage walls made them unsuitable for supporting shelves or heavy built-in cupboards.

Left: A skillfully carved armoire in oak from Normandy with a floral theme. The central upright is faux-dormant, and inside there are three shelves, the lowest of which carries two drawers. 86" x 56". $3200 - 6400

The top of this glazed oak armoire carries a Celtic-looking frieze which looks Breton. In fact, it comes from Normandy.

The elliptical medallions on each door are key Norman characteristics. $3200 - 6400

A close up of the doors shows the tops of the mixte panels (turned on one side only) and the medallions. The rich oak color blends successfully with a collection of blue plates.

Elaborate carving is a distinctive feature of Norman work, especially in the region's most representative piece, the armoire. Prosperity and love were the key decorative themes of the eighteenth and nineteenth centuries, with cornucopiae, grapes, wheat sheaves and flowers conveying the former, while hearts, arrows, quivers and billing doves symbolized the latter. Other typical designs included acanthus leaves, geometric patterns, farm implements, musical instruments and anchors.

Cornices were flat, or from the late eighteenth century rounded upward in a *châpeau de gendarme* or policeman's hat shape, usually decorated with lavish three-dimensional carving.

The Norman armoire features decorative metalwork, mainly of wrought iron until the mid-nineteenth century and later in copper or brass. A sculpted pilaster runs down the center of eighteenth and nineteenth century examples and occasionally there is a drawer in the base. Feet are usually curved, perhaps with snail shells and little sabots.

A significant characteristic is the richness of carving on the central traverses of the doors, with an elliptical medallion, either vertical or at an angle, as its most frequent motif.

The Norman vaisselier is usually made in oak, elm, cherry or pine, with a straight cornice and shelves with sculpted railings to hold faience and porcelain. Sometimes hooks are also fitted to hang cider cups. It sits normally on a buffet which has two square, ornamented doors and shortish, curved legs.

Tables are distinctive because of their thick tops and sturdy proportions. In oak or elm, with four or six strong square legs, they often have sliding shelves. Traditionally, they were accompanied by simple, long benches.

Chairs were heavily influenced by the style of Louis XV and were often upholstered. Classic high back chairs featured rush seats and three undulating rungs on the backs.

Buffets à deux corps were created primarily for dining rooms and, unlike armoires, were kept comparatively simple in design. Often the top section was notably taller and narrower than the base, and occasionally the top was also glazed.

The Normans' reputation for hospitality is demonstrated by the regional popularity of extending tables, here with a small single drawer at the side, slightly shaped legs and doe feet. *Courtesy of Palmer Antiques.* $4000-5600

Fully extended on pull-out supports, this table adds 30" to its normal 70". *Courtesy of Palmer Antiques.*

This unusual buffet has pierced sheet-iron panels and a marble top. Made in the Avranches region it is called an armoirette de laiterie, and was made originally for a dairy to store and cut cheese. *Courtesy of Dudley Hume Antiques.* $4800-6400

A classic of Norman furniture is the grandfather clock, either with a straight-sided casing or a demoiselle hour-glass shape which has a glazed middle portion to allow movement for the pendulum. Most famed by name are the clocks of Saint-Nicolas d'Aliermont, which are extremely tall, narrow and heavily carved round the face.

Upholstery was favored by Norman craftsmen for their simplified versions of Louis XV and Louis XVI style chaises. *Courtesy of Palmer Antiques.* $1200-2400

Left: A strong fruitwood and oak table with a single drawer. The usual simple steel button has been replaced but the overall effect is not spoiled. $1200-2800

Popularity of the single or low buffet became widespread in the nineteenth century, especially in the Eure region. As in other parts of France it proved a practical choice for storage, especially linen, at a manageable price. This two-door buffet with no drawers is in strongly figured pine. This wood was often used in Normandy, but the home grown product, knotty and resinous, was often combined with imported pine, especially in the maritime regions of Upper Normandy. Slightly red in color, it was easier to carve. *Courtesy of Gloucester House Antiques.* $4000-5600

Right: Is it a tall buffet or a small armoire? An armoirette is perhaps the best description, made here to a simple design in cherrywood. *Courtesy of Gloucester House Antiques.* $4000-5600

The unusual pattern on the door tops lifts the look of this otherwise straightforward pine buffet. *Courtesy of Gloucester House Antiques.* $4800-6400

Don't be misled by the sober styling of this small oak buffet. It is just as Norman as the more exuberant creations, but harks back to the rectilinear look of its seventeenth century forebear, the coffer. *Courtesy of Gloucester House Antiques.* $4000-5000

Left: Necessity is often the mother of invention, and when the more wealthy households needed to put an additional coffer of linen on top of another, but also wanted ready access to both, the double buffet was created with doors at the front instead of lids on top. Most were plain in appearance, like the examples from nearby Brittany, but others were designed to accompany an armoire, and were just as heavily ornamented. This example in pine features one of the most popular motifs in Normandy, a pair of birds, carved in high relief to symbolize love, marriage and fidelity. It was particularly favored in the Caux region, to the north east of Normandy. *Courtesy of Gloucester House Antiques.* $4800-7200

A wonderfully ornate pine double buffet with glazed doors for display and an elaborate châpeau de gendarme cornice. *Courtesy of Gloucester House Antiques.* $8000-9600

Below: The glazed central upright and the mannered cornice add sophistication to this otherwise simple double buffet. *Courtesy of Gloucester House Antiques.* $5600-7200

Provincial decorations tend to represent the actual aspirations of their owners. Shells symbolize fertility; grapes or ears of corn, productive farming; fruit or flowers, divine grace; and musical instruments, artistic accomplishment. They can also indicate where pieces came from. The floral basket, for example, was particularly popular in Calvados. Here, these finely carved panels express the hope that the land will yield an abundance of food. *Courtesy of Gloucester House Antiques.* $8000-9600

Left: Some experts claim to have identified a link between the ornamental pieces made near the major part of Cherbourg and the carvings of the Far East. Certainly, the frieze-like qualities of the abundant floral work on this buffet recall the Orient. *Courtesy of Gloucester House Antiques.* $4000-5600

Usually the top half of a Norman double buffet is narrower than the bottom. This one is in oak. *Courtesy of Gloucester House Antiques.* $4000-5600

A handsome oak double buffet with châpeau de gendarme cornice and narrow carved feet. The wood in the panels is similar to that found in the Caen, Rouen and Caux regions. Famous for centuries it is broadly veined and gives a shimmering effect like moiré silk. *Courtesy of Gloucester House Antiques.* $6400-8000

The Cauchoise armoire, from the Caux region, is easily identified by its distinctive elliptical medallions on the doors. The style, also followed in the adjoining Caen and Pays d'Auge regions, usually involves richly carved decoration in the medallions. This oak armoire could come from Flers, slightly further south, where gardening motifs symbolizing work were popular and led to their armoires being called jardinières. The cornice features a 'pelican' entwining motif representing family devotion, often seen on buffet doors. *Courtesy of Gloucester House Antiques.* $8000-9600

Attention to detail is often exceptional in Norman work. This armoire features delicate low relief carvings on the mid-panel traverses and startlingly ornate feet. *Courtesy of Gloucester Antiques.* $8000-9600

Left: Normandy folk were particularly attracted to the symbols of the Louis XVI era which evoked marriage and conjugal happiness - entwined hearts, the flame, a quiver and arrows, and, as on this oak armoire, a pair of lovebirds. Such themes were considered particularly appropriate for the most important piece of furniture in the home, and the one with which a young couple would start their married life. *Courtesy of Gloucester House Antiques.* $8000-9600

Left: Floral decorations, but with an unusual treatment of the central medallions. *Courtesy of Gloucester House Antiques.*

Left: A simple light oak armoire. Strict laws governed the use of wood. It was forbidden to use green wood and a minimum drying out period of seven years was set by law. Clearly, the rules were interpreted in line with prevailing local custom. *Courtesy of Gloucester House Antiques.* $5600-7200

An attractive pine armoire. Norman furniture was designed for dismantling and, if necessary, a piece like this could be easily unpinned and carried up a narrow stairway. 92" x 52" x 19.5" *Courtesy of Gloucester House Antiques.* $5600-7200

Left: Oak again, this time with plenty of entwining pelican symbols. *Courtesy of Gloucester House Antiques.* $6400-8000

Blonde oak gives this armoire a fresh look like pearwood. 79" x 50" x 18". *Courtesy of Gloucester House Antiques.* $5600-7200

Restrained but effective ornamentation on a pine armoire. *Courtesy of Gloucester House Antiques.* $5600-7200

The Normans called their dressers paliers rather than vaisseliers as elsewhere. Unexpectedly, in a region rich in faience it is not the most common piece of furniture. *Courtesy of Gloucester House Antiques.* $4800-7200

This oak Buffet à Deux Corps could have been made at any time during the nine-teenth century. $4800-6400

In fact, its date was carved discreetly on the inside top of the right hand side door.

Brittany

Brittany is France's Celtic fringe; a wild and poetic region which has much in common with Ireland or Wales.

The heavy Atlantic seas break onto the rocky headlands of this remote peninsula, France's westernmost corner, and desolate moors run down to coastal plains. Curious, carved stone shrines in the villages are visual reminders of the region's religious beliefs, linked to an historic awe of the sea.

The region's furniture is as distinctive as its special culture. Overall it combines magnitude with a squareness of shape and richness in decoration that brings in geometric, floral, animal or human motifs in an original and imaginative country style.

The Bretons have always displayed a great love of ornamentation, and often they have been unable to resist adding their chiselled details to a piece made for them by a local joiner. The results can be a delightfully naive combination of the practical and the whimsical.

The fruitwood farmhouse table was made in the south of Brittany and dates from the 1770s. The walnut dining chairs, circa 1820, are from Provence. Courtesy of L'Encoignure, London. Table $6400-9600, chairs $3200-4000 for six

A Breton vaisselier distinguished by busy ornamentation and balustraded shelves. Since the decorations on the rack and the buffet base are the same it is almost certain that the two sections were made for each other; not always the case in a region where racks were more frequent and buffets were sometimes married to them. $4000-7200

Essentially, carving tends to be in light relief, with mainly rectilinear edges - even Louis XV's strong influence failed to convert most outlines, apart from those of the feet.

There are two geographical styles - the Lower Breton and the Upper Breton. In Lower Brittany, especially in Finistère, the lines are straighter and stricter. In Upper Brittany, a closer neighbour to Normandy and the Loire, the styles are more elegant and contoured, with occasional Louis XV or Louis XVI influences visible in the ornamentation.

It is Lower Brittany which expresses best the true character of the region, with its squarer, more robust pieces. Today such pieces by themselves look strong and commanding in a room setting, but when they were made the fashion was to line up furniture as an ensemble, and it was not uncommon to see a large room with two identical armoires on either side of a similarly contructed bed.

The Breton armoire is therefore either very simple or decorated vividly with allegorical scenes or motifs. The enthusiastic Breton carvers preferred stylised floral bouquets and branches, interlacing geometrical patterns, religious emblems, animals, human figures, village scenes, marriages, dances or episodes from the histories of the saints!

Perhaps the finest armoires were made around Rennes, where skilled carvers featured fruit, flowers and birds in symmetrical patterns on armoires made in oak, chestnut or cherry, often with double châpeau de gendarmes, or crossbow shaped, cornices.

One particularly unusual style of armoire emanates from the Guérande district. Rectangular in shape, with two doors each containing three decorated panels, the center pair with circles and the remainder with large pointed diamonds, this armoire was usually painted a vivid red. Now attractively faded, such pieces are rare.

Few full-scale vaisseliers were made in Brittany, and simple draining or plate racks were more common, often made to be hung on the wall over a buffet, particularly in the Morbihan region. Typically, they had balustraded galleries to keep the plates in position.

Traditional tables often look like thin coffers set on legs with decorative work along the sides. Tables from Rennes are more elegant, with hints of Louis XIII style, while the Guérande table has turned feet and a turned stretcher with a small vase in the center, the ensemble painted red to match the armoire.

The typical Breton seat is the bench, rustic and simple, and the indispensable accompaniment to any table.

The buffet was not introduced until comparatively late, and usually reflects the rectangular shapes of the Lower Brittany armoires, although the buffets of Ile-et-Vilaine are more elegant, with detectable influences of Louis XV, Louis XVI and even Directoire and Empire periods. The buffets of Morbihan are distinguished by ornamentation over large sections and by the long and elaborate steel escutcheons.

Clocks are also often squarish, with ornamentation and primitive marquetry in the Morbihan and festoons after Louis XV in the Rennes area.

The double châpeau de gendarme declares this to be a fine armoire from Rennes with the distinctive light relief carving of the area. *Courtesy of Gloucester House Antiques.* $5600-7200

A vaisselier-égouttoir from Ile-et-Vilaine made in cherry to a very distinctive design featuring playing card motifs and some marquetry. Versions from the Morbihan area were made to be hung on walls. 85" x 45" x 9.5". *Courtesy of Gloucester House Antiques.* $9600-11,200

Left: A Lower Breton armoire with typically square outline and an integral cornice. *Courtesy of Gloucester House Antiques.* $4000-5000

Below: Breton armoires were often intended to be lined up on either side of beds against a wall, and it was not always felt necessary to make sides for their cornices. This four-square example, dated 1893, has no cornice at all, but an abundance of decorative marquetry and metalwork offsets the solid construction. Typically, the doors do not go right to the bottom and two horizontal panels are set in to create a kind of shallow coffer in the base. *Courtesy of Gloucester House Antiques.* $4800-6400

Another Rennes armoire, this time with the decorative emphasis on the four chantourné panels. The simple carving repeats the whimsical, allegorical Celtic motifs which appear on pottery, jewelry and shrines. *Courtesy of Gloucester House Antiques.* $5600-7200

Buffets and double buffets became popular in Brittany later than in some regions and do not present any particular regional characteristics. This one, in chestnut, is simple in style but distinguished by striking brass escutcheons. *Courtesy of Gloucester House Antiques.* $4800-6400

Right: Breton tables often look like coffers on legs. The decorated front and turned legs suggest this one comes from Rennes. A pair of panels slide back so that plates and cutlery can be stored inside between meals. *Courtesy of Gloucester House Antiques.* $4800-6400

Left: A rustic pine buffet with glazed top for storage and display. 84" x 58" x 20". *Courtesy of Gloucester House Antiques.* $4000-5600

Above: A simpler table from Nantes with a single drawer at the end, used, in this case, for storing bread. *Courtesy of Gloucester House Antiques.* $3200-4800

Left: A very unusual food cupboard in cherry. The Morbihan district favored cherry along with chestnut, walnut and pear. In Cornouaille, oak, chestnut, walnut and fruitwood for small pieces were preferred, while around Léon the choice was dark oak. *Courtesy of Gloucester House Antiques.* $4800-7200

A glazed walnut food cupboard with drawers demonstrating versatility by displaying books, pottery and magazines. *Courtesy of Gloucester House Antiques.* $4800-7200

Right: The profusion of carving on this cherry buffet points to this being a Breton piece. Finely finished keyhole surrounds enhance its exceptional quality. *Courtesy of Gloucester House Antiques.* $4800-7200

Loire Valley

The Loire Valley is France's fairytale country. Mile upon mile of castles are set like pearls in a lush green countryside, punctuated by splendid forests and neat vineyards.

Numerous royal palaces were established in the Loire over the centuries, and these regal connections resulted in a quality in the construction of local furniture that sets it apart.

A quest for harmony of form and finesse in execution are clearly evident, as is the direct influence of fashionable styles of the time. The introduction of Renaissance decor left an early imprint, especially on the work of Orléans and Touraine, but it was Louis XV, inevitably, who had the greatest impact.

It is quite apparent in the magnificent armoires of Touraine, fashioned from walnut or cherry and glistening with enormous hinges of steel or copper. Inside, there are often two compartments separated by a drawer. The equally beautiful armoires from Maine can be distinguished by the crossbow shaped cornicing, in the Rennes manner.

Tables are rectangular with turned legs connected by H- or X-shaped stretchers.

While benches are few and far between in the Orléans area, they are more than made up for in the Touraine, where they are often long enough to seat eight people at a time. Everywhere there can be found a huge range of chairs and armchairs in poplar or birch, usually with rushing.

Left: A cherry armoire typifying the sophisticated style and finish of Loire furniture. *Courtesy of Gloucester House Antiques.* $5600-7200

A more rustic light walnut two-drawer buffet. *Courtesy of Gloucester House Antiques.* $4000-5600

A light oak buffet à deux corps with full-length steel hinges and discreet, refined styling. *Courtesy of Gloucester House Antiques.* $4800-7200

Right: Walnut and oak combined in a buffet with keyhole surrounds reminiscent of those from the Vendeé. Larger versions with more than two doors were also made. *Courtesy of Gloucester House Antiques.* $4000-5600

Nineteenth century buffets à deux corps made between Tours and Angers have slender top sections and discreet ornamentation, while the versions from Orléans have prominent arched cornices and those from Anjou are often decorated with deeply carved diamonds. Just about every type of wood was used.

Right: A fine example of provincial craftsmanship. Urban influences modified, here in cherry, to impart a country feel. *Courtesy of Gloucester House Antiques.* $4800-7200

A good quality oak commode from the northern Val de Loire. 32" x 36" x 23". *Courtesy of Gloucester House Antiques.* $4800-7200

A late eighteenth century commode in elm. *Courtesy of Gloucester House Antiques.* $5600-8000

Left: A finely-detailed cherry draining rack converted for storage by adding a plank base. *Courtesy of Gloucester House Antiques.* $1600-2400

63

Poitou, Vendée and Saintonge

This large region is regarded by some as the spiritual home of classic provincial furniture. For here, more than anywhere, the craftsmen, carpenters, joiners and artisans achieved a subtle balance between the fashionably stylish and the basically rustic, with local characteristics still in evidence.

The Poitou, the Vendée and the Saintonge comprise together a substantial area of France which combines agricultural land with prosperous towns, and the region's central position geographically has always made it receptive to influences from all around.

Its furniture echoes this sensitivity by presenting a look that is a pure harmony of town and country.

The enormous selection of available woods was also made full use of. In the Vendée you will find cherry, chestnut, ash and pear; in Poitou, cherry, white walnut and burr elm; in the Saintonge, cherry, chestnut and burr ash. Often, contrasting panels were set into the doors and moldings in black or brown were added to create rich visual

A rare walnut commode from the Charente area of Poitou, circa 1770. Its serpentine shape echoes the styles of the South. *Courtesy of L'Encoignure, London.* $9500-12,000

An unusually wide Vendeé armoire in cherrywood, one of the most popular woods of the region. 83″ x 56″ x 24″ *Courtesy of Gloucester House Antiques*

A dream find from the Vendée, a matching armoire and buffet with chantourné panels and brass escutcheons with plenty of impact. *Courtesy of Gloucester House Antiques.* $16,000-19,200

You would have to go to Burgundy, or especially Bresse, to find such a profusion of armoires. This example, in walnut, uses elegantly molded panels to achieve its effect. *Courtesy of Gloucester House Antiques.* $4800-6400

An unusual cross between an armoire and a buffet à deux corps. Narrow snake-like escutcheons such as these were often used on early furniture. *Courtesy of Gloucester House Antiques.* $4000-5600

A cherrywood armoire in the sober style that typifies the region. *Courtesy of Gloucester House Antiques.* $4800-6400

confections of color and grain. Decorations used in this region typify the ornamentation of provincial furniture throughout France, and are worth listing. Shaped moldings around panels and doors were the principal decorative element of all furniture inspired by Louis XIII and Louis XV styles, and were *chantourné*, that is, turned on all sides, *demi-chantourné*, turned on two sides, or *mixte*, turned on one side only.

Discs, circles or gateaux were a popular and often repeated motif on armoires, while diamonds, the Maltese Cross and the Cross of Saint-André were equally favored, especially in the West and South West, often mixed with circles and lozenge shapes.

Flora, fauna and human figures replaced the former after Louis XV, when garlands and foliage were used to decorate panels and the edges of moldings. Bouquets, vine branches and birds also found a place on cornices and crosspieces and after Louis XVI new motifs appeared, among them quivers, arrows, flames, crowns, urns and ribbon bows.

Polished metalwork became an increasingly important visual element during the seventeenth century, and furniture in the spirit of Louis XIII and Louis XIV was embellished with two or three steel hinges, though with a comparatively small escutcheon.

Following Louis XV's reign the hinges grew to occupy the entire height of the doors, while escutcheons also became dramatically elongated, often with intricate patterns cut through them.

Smart yet rustic. A well-made small cherrywood armoire that defines the region's harmonious balance of town and country. *Courtesy of Gloucester House Antiques.* $5600-8000

Left: A tiny face is carved into the center of the frieze. It could have been the maker or the owner-to-be. *Courtesy of Gloucester House Antiques.* $5600-8000

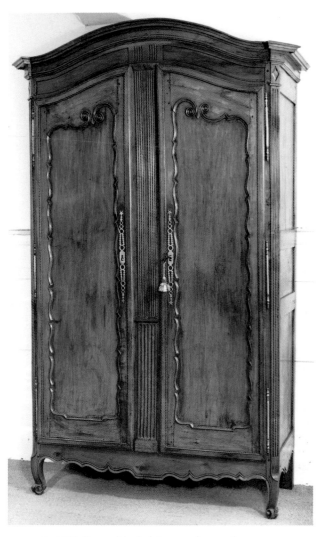

A skillfully molded châpeau de gendarme cornice, chantourné panels, a mixture of stylistic influences plus eye-catching brasswork make this a typically assured example. In cherry, from the Vendeé. *Courtesy of Gloucester House Antiques.* $6400-8000

This is genuinely cherry, but sometimes poplar was stained to take on a similar color. *Courtesy of Gloucester House Antiques.* $4000-5600

Quite a sophisticated marriage armoire from Nantes with dramatic configurations on the door panels to represent hearts. 92" x 51" x 20". *Courtesy of Gloucester House Antiques.* $6400-8000

Although the periods of Louis XVI, the Empire and Restoration saw a fashionable Paris movement towards the minimal in terms of metalwork, the country craftsmen continued to favour the tradition of exaggerated escutcheons, often in copper or burnished brass. In the coastal Vendée, for example, the trend was to lengthen the design even further by adding stars, urns or hooks to the ends.

The abundance of armoires in certain parts of the Vendée, particularly the Marais, can be explained by the simple fact that the adobe walls would not hold shelves.

Diamonds and circles may well have gained particular popularity as favoured motifs before spreading to other parts of the country, since the Vendée was an important staging post between the Loire and the deep South. The advent of more intricate rococo ornamentation brought an increasingly curvaceous look linked to a new adventurousness in the use of contrasting woods. Most popular for everyday use were cherry and walnut.

There is no doubt that the perfect piece of furniture to display porcelain or majolica is a vaisselier, and the Vendée produced a wide range of alternative designs. Sometimes a vaisselier was conceived and made as a whole, but, as often as not, it was made in the form of a buffet-vaisselier, consisting of two parts, a buffet as the base and a shelving unit above with long runners at the bottom through which it could be fixed to the buffet top. Each shelf has a simple bar in contrast to the balustraded style of Brittany. Favoured woods were cherry in the Marais and speckled elm in the Fontenay and Luçon.

Oak, young elm and cherry were the popular choices for tables, which sometimes have a compartment at one end to hold tablecloths.

The rising curve of the doors, panels turned on all four sides and lively brass lock surrounds give this cherry armoire plenty of character. *Courtesy of Gloucester House Antiques.* $6400-8000

Below: The cabinet is something of a speciality of the region. It is also known as a narrow buffet and can be found with two doors, or more commonly, with one, as in this example in cherry. *Courtesy of Gloucester House Antiques.* $4000-5600

This is the two-door version, in this case with a drawer between. Again in cherry, and with the lack of ornamentation that is typical of cabinets from the Vendeé. *Courtesy of Gloucester House Antiques.* $4800-6400

In some parts of the Vendeé this type of cabinet is nicknamed 'l'homme debout', which can be translated as 'the upright man'. *Courtesy of Gloucester House Antiques.* $4000-5600

The cabinets of Saintonge are slightly larger than those of the Vendeé or Poitou. This one, in cherry, sports an elaborate open-work escutcheon in a popular regional style. *Courtesy of Gloucester House Antiques.* $4800-6400

Chairs are normally rush seated with ladder backs, turned arms and double stretchers for strength.

By comparison, buffets were the subject of some inventiveness, as successive craftsmen gradually extended them in length from the original two door style to models with as many as five doors. These became known as enfilades or buffets Nantais.

Buffets à deux corps come in numerous variations, and there is often a considerable difference in proportion between the two halves, especially among the versions which have simply designed panelling. Either the top is considerably set back from the base at the front, or the sides are much narrower. Often the apparent imbalance adds a charm which a more proportionate version would lack.

Clocks are also distinctive, their dials painted with brightly colored flowers or, unusually, made in mahogany, thanks to the proximity of the port of Nantes.

In keeping with the region's ancient reputation as an innovator is the occasional appearance of a local commode, a rare piece in country terms in most other regions. In the Ile-de-Noirmoutier, for instance, they made serpentine fronted chests of drawers with swan neck handles and doe feet.

The buffet-vaisselier of the Vendeé always looks as if it was not conceived as a single entity. The single plate rack has two elongated feet with which to attach it to a normal buffet, its only concession to unity!
Courtesy of Gloucester House Antiques.
$4800-6400

The racks are usually simple with straight bars to hold crockery, unlike the elaborate turnings preferred in Brittany. A distinctive feature, however, is the long, turned button hanging from each front end of the cornice. *Courtesy of Gloucester House Antiques.* $4800-6400

Most buffet-vaisseliers are made in cherrywood. *Courtesy of Gloucester House Antiques.* $4800-6400

Left: Often in cherry, the buffets are generally simple in ornamentation and it is in the details that their characters come through. Here, a single small drawer is set above the faux dormant. *Courtesy of Gloucester House Antiques.* $4000-5600

Left: In a typical country interior of the region the buffet vaisselier would be placed on the wall facing the fireplace, with an armoire on either side. If a second room was used for meals another buffet vaisselier would be positioned next to a round table and chairs. *Courtesy of Gloucester House Antiques.* $4800-6400

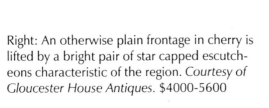

Right: An otherwise plain frontage in cherry is lifted by a bright pair of star capped escutcheons characteristic of the region. *Courtesy of Gloucester House Antiques.* $4000-5600

The use of multi-shaded walnut distinguishes this two-drawer buffet. *Courtesy of Gloucester House Antiques.* $4000-5600

The region's size and position caused it to be influenced stylistically by both the North and the South. This walnut buffet's plain upper section is supported by a vivacious lower traverse and feet that look more typical of the Languedoc or Provence. *Courtesy of Gloucester House Antiques.* $4800-6400

Right: Oak, found principally in the Angoumois, is used for this sturdy buffet de chasse. Used for cutting up game it would normally have a marble top. *Courtesy of Gloucester House Antiques.* $4800-6400

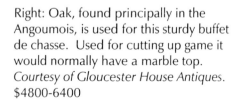

Right: The buffet à deux corps is one of the key pieces of the Vendée, along with the enfilade and the cabinet. A huge variation of styles and proportions can be found. This one, with a combination of stylistic influences (note the unusual feet) is in cherry. *Courtesy of Gloucester House Antiques.* $4000-6400

Taller and narrower than usual, this two-door buffet is in walnut and comes from Poitou. *Courtesy of Gloucester House Antiques.* $4000-5600

Left: The buffet enfilade or nantais, these come in three, four and even five-door versions. The four-door style often looks like a pair of buffets joined together, and the door panels are sometimes different in style. *Courtesy of Palmer Antiques.* $4800-6400

The use of burr ash and some simple but effective marquetry makes this Vendée buffet particularly striking. *Courtesy of Gloucester House Antiques.* $4800-6000

Right: A lovely eighteenth century fruitwood double buffet. Often the upper section was much narrower than the lower. *Courtesy of Gloucester House Antiques.* $9600-11,200

Clock cases were decorated with marquetry in the Saintonge and were given delicate feet. *Courtesy of Gloucester House Antiques.* $3200-4000

Left: A tall clock in a wood case would be placed in the main room of most houses from the nineteenth century onwards. *Courtesy of Gloucester House Antiques.* $3200-4000

A rare piece in mahogany from Bordeaux. It seems to be a close relative of the ornamental panetière or bread box from Provence, but simpler in style. Mahogany, imported from overseas, was used occasionally by craftsmen working close to major ports. *Courtesy of Gloucester House Antiques.* $3200-4800

Country sophistication at its best. A very pretty cherrywood buffet with elegantly molded chantourné panels and delicate floral motifs. *Courtesy of Gloucester House Antiques.* $5600-7200

Right: An attractive dark cherry cabinet in the style of Louis XVI. 74" x 34" x 22". *Courtesy of Gloucester House Antiques.* $5600-7200

Basque and Béarn

Walnut, fruitwoods and oak were preferred in the region, but pine was also used, here in a nineteenth century dresser decorated with rural patterns. Local name for a dresser is a bacheratéguy. *Courtesy of Gloucester House Antiques.* $4800-6400

Endless golden beaches flanked by thick forests studded with glittering lakes. Add some strong breezes and the powerful presence of the Atlantic Ocean and you are in the Béarn and Basque country, with Spain just a few kilometres due south.

The local cheeses, Poustagnac, Arneguy and Iraty, are little known outside the region, and the furniture is encountered as infrequently.

The Basque region has three ancient provences: Soule, Lower Navarre and Labourd. The first prefers oak, the second wild cherry, chestnut, pear, apple and walnut, and the last, oak and walnut. In the Béarn, oak and walnut are favoured.

Metalwork is reduced to a minimum; there are no elongated or elaborate escutcheons here. But ornamentation is energetically conceived to represent fans, circles, rosettes, pierced hearts or blooms like the marguerite, fittingly the flower of the sun. As in Brittany, religious emblems are everywhere: crosses, chalices, monstrances, hearts with sunbeams, and alongside them, representations of the sun, the moon and stars and even the swastika in its original form as a magic symbol.

Armoires from the Béarn can be identified by their decoration with the Maltese Cross or fleur de lys, while Basque examples often have diamond point ornamentation and a large drawer in the base. The carving is deep, direct and vigorous.

Buffets-vaisselier, usually in cherry, have three drawers in the base and little cupboards on either side of the upper sections.

Tables are large and rectangular with double-T stretchers and two or three drawers.

Chairs are Spanish influenced, straight angled, trapeze shaped and only turned on the feet or stretchers. Armchairs and stools may be leather covered.

Clocks are very rare in this region, as are the small pieces which are plentiful in some other parts.

Right: These two side cabinets, waiting for their tops to be replaced after restoration, look capable of walking thanks to their maker's interpretation of Louis XV style legs. $1200-1600

Leather covering reflects the Spanish influence on the region. The chairs are in walnut. *Courtesy of Palmer Antiques.* $3200-4000

Right: A simple side table in walnut. $400-1200

A real rarity, this nineteenth century provincial bureau. Most bureaux were city-made and declared their origins by elaborate veneers, marquetry and ormolu trimmings. $2400-3200

Made in walnut, a bureau like this would have looked in keeping with simple furnishings in warm southern colors. $2400-4000

Languedoc and Roussillon

Botanists love the Languedoc for its rugged, hidden parts and rare plants.

Perhaps this region still harbors some rare flowers in furniture terms, since it has for long been overshadowed by its neighbour, Provence.

For the pieces created in the Nîmes region represent as rich a selection of materials and as perfect an attention to line as those produced across the border in Arles.

You can find, as in Provence, the panetière for bread, although the pétrin does not appear to have been made here. Towards Narbonne and Perpignan outlines are heavier, in keeping with Spanish Catalan style, but elsewhere shapes are curved and rounded.

Buffets à deux corps are rare, but single buffets are plentiful, as are armoires. Commodes were also produced in great numbers and in a variety of styles, from rustic to bourgeois. The preferred woods were walnut, occasionally elm and sometimes fruitwoods like wild cherry, apple or pear.

As in other parts of France, the armoire represents the defining spirit of the region, and here the richness and voluptuousness of the ornamentation declares it instantly to be a product of the Latin south.

A walnut two-drawer commode in the Languedoc manner, circa 1770. A pair of early to mid-nineteenth century walnut fauteuils. *Courtesy of L'Encoignure, London.* Commode $6400-9600, fauteuils $4000-6500

A richly decorated two-drawer commode in wild cherry from Nîmes. Its curvaceous outline, busy carving and pretty metalwork are typical of work from this part of the country. *Courtesy of Gloucester House Antiques.* $8000-9600

An early eighteenth century Languedoc commode in cherry. A wide range of local commodes was made in two, three and four-drawer versions, sometimes with gently curved, but otherwise plain, drawers which relied on decorative metalwork for their visual impact, although the lower traverse often featured carved work along its entire length and onto the feet. *Courtesy of Gloucester House Antiques.* $11,200-14,400

A fine example which I glimpsed through the window of a home near Toulouse was distinguished by four symmetrical panels lavishly molded on every side, richly carved ornamentation in Louis XV style all round the doors and an elaborate shell cartouche at the center of the châpeau de gendarme cornice. Created in rich walnut, it would have looked as much at home in a field of sunflowers as it did in the study of this house.

Chairs are rush seated, and for the first time, travelling South East, you find examples of the long setee, often wide enough for three or four people sitting side by side.

For some reason clocks are almost non-existent in this region.

Spanish Catalan influence can be seen in the exaggerated front skirt and legs of this otherwise simple pine table. $1280-1440.

Long rush-seated settees, often big enough to seat four people were made to accommodate the sociable habits of the people of Languedoc, just as they were in Provence. $3200-4800

Auvergne

Travelling North and inland from the Languedoc you reach a region of mountains and forests which long remained undisturbed by the currents of trend and fashion.

In the days before modern transport, the deeply canyoned Auvergne proved impenetrable to all but the most determined travellers and communications remained sparse. The rugged individuality which resulted from this isolation is reflected in the robust and calm appeal of many auvergnat pieces.

Deep, straight carving is a feature of the region, as are the objects and small pieces of furniture which were often created at home during dark winter nights. Decorated with an array of motifs - zigzags, lozenges, rosettes, checkers, stars and countless geometric patterns - they typify the look of the Auvergne.

There was never a shortage of wood here, and a beautiful red walnut was most often selected for furniture-making, together with chestnut. In most areas, fruitwood was favored. Velay is noted for cherry, apple, pear and lime; Dômes for wild cherry. Beech was reserved for chair-making.

Steel and copper were produced for handles, hinges and escutcheons, with Cantal becoming known as the center for the best copper work.

The Buffet à Deux Corps comes from the Auvergne and is in merisier. It was made in the late eighteenth century. The fruitwood extending dining table is circa 1800. *Courtesy of L'Encoignure, London.* Buffet $6400-9600

Here, the communal living room was traditionally at the heart of family life, and an array of fine armoires would often be found at the end of this room. Less popular than the buffet in this region, most were in a simplified Louis XV style with curved snail shell feet and two doors sometimes with large, protruding drawers in the base.

Buffets are far more numerous, not only single and à deux corps, but also in tall one-piece versions sometimes with open balustrade doors in the top sections to make a food cupboard.

The artisans of the Auvergne were often late in assimilating stylistic influences but when they did they amalgamated the various features around their own distinctive look. Thus it is not rare to find pieces which are dominated by the geometric ornamentation of the region, yet are supplemented by cambered Louis XV feet, fluted Louis XVI columns and a large, protruding Louis XIII cornice.

Cherrywood from Velay gives color and depth to a simply structured two-door, two-drawer buffet. Made in the late nineteenth century in an earlier style. $800-1280.

The low ceilings of homes in the region often meant that cornices were dispensed with and proportions adjusted to give more width and less height. This oak armoire has the typical square look of pieces from the Auvergne, with only the metalwork, door moldings and apron shaping to relieve the severe lines. *Courtesy of Gloucester House Antiques.* $4000-5600

Provence

The warm blue Mediterranean sea which washes the beaches of Provence has played its own special part in making Provençal furniture among the most appealing to come out of France.

The naval establishments in its main ports and the river trade generated around the Rhône which flows into it made Provence a prosperous area, and one which demanded furniture to match its opulence at all levels of society.

The local artisans responded with true exuberance, and when they discovered Louis XV style the scene was set for an epoch of unrestrained yet skilled furniture-making.

The carpenters of Provence seized every opportunity to express themselves and their ranges of buffets and armoires were augmented by equally appealing smaller pieces with specific functions, such as the bread holder, salt box and flour box.

Earlier, simple regional styles had developed, notably around Avignon and Toulon, where naval officers supported the establishment of furniture makers.

But the romanticism of Louis XV marked a major development, coming as it did as the local economy boomed and the wealthy residents of Arles, Beaucaire and Tarascon began to seek furniture for their new homes.

A pair of lovebirds is featured in the exceptional carving on this walnut armoire from Arles, circa 1775. The walnut fauteuil dates from 1740. *Courtesy of L'Encoignure, London.* Armoire $12,000-19,000, fauteuil $4500-8000

This pine buffet is deeply carved with floral motifs in a style echoing the lively work of Normandy and Brittany. $4000-4800

The Provençal canapé or radassié, pictured here prior to re-rushing, has eight legs like its Languedoc neighbor. *Courtesy of Palmer Antiques.*

The distinctive radassié with its new rushing. *Courtesy of Palmer Antiques.* $4000-5600

Two styles soon began to develop; that of Arles and that of Fourques. Both used similar overall forms, but the decoration differed. Pieces from Arles are more eleborate, offering ornate carvings, curved lines and rich details with the emphasis on low-relief floral themes such as garlands of roses, flower buds and olive branches.

Those from Fourques are less decorated and can be identified by deeply sculpted curves, undulating moldings and a more architectural appearance.

Provençal craftsmen had another significant advantage. The local wood available to them had a rich, glowing, honey-toned patina which would only improve with age. Light, golden walnut, once abundant, was favoured, along with exotic local timber from olive trees, pear, willow, cherry, chestnut and mulberry.

If Normandy has a competitor in the armoire stakes, it must be Provence. The southern artisans created voluminous, richly decorated cupboards with two or perhaps three undulating panels per door, lavishly carved borders and ornate metalwork running from top to bottom of the doors.

Lacy, symmetrical escutcheons were placed one on top of the other, up to three at a time, along the length of doors and drawers, picking up the light and creating an intricate and dramatic embellishment.

A walnut pétrin with hinged top. They were often wedding gifts. $400-800

Smartly upholstered in ticking, this is Provence's interpretation of the chaise longue, here made from fruitwood in the eighteenth century. $4800-6400

Gently serpentine in shape, this cherrywood commode is richly embellished with decorative handles and escutcheons. 38" x 50" x 20". $1600-4000

Not all Provençal work was elaborate. This painted pine cupboard was made originally for a simple country home. *Courtesy of Palmer Antiques.* $3200-4800

A variation on the long rushed seat, this one is like two chairs facing each other. *Courtesy of Palmer Antiques.* $2400-3200

Another painted cupboard, this one could have been made for the kitchen of a townhouse. *Courtesy of Palmer Antiques.* $3200-4800

The most sought-after armoires today are those from Saint-Rémy, Beaucaire and Arles. Versions from further North, beyond the Comtat region, are simpler and more sculptured.

Provençal artisans also distinguished themselves by producing several pieces which are unique to their part of France. The buffet à glissants is a two-tiered storage cabinet emanating from Haute Provence and featuring a traditional buffet base topped by a small, separate upper section with two sliding doors. This unusual design was conceived so that glasses could be taken out of the top part without disturbing vases or containers sitting on the buffet top.

The encoignure is another local inspiration: a tall, narrow, three-sided cabinet, sometimes bowfronted, made specifically to be placed in the corner of a room.

A rare piece today is the manjadou, a one-piece cupboard with a single door, the top half of which has elaborately turned spindles to allow the air to circulate inside and permit it to be used for food storage. There is often a single drawer at the bottom.

Also typically Provençal is the panetière, a richly ornamented little cupboard on small legs with escargot feet. Its front has similarly turned spindles to the manjadou, and more spindles rise from the top as pure decoration. Its purpose is to hold freshly baked bread and despite its feet it is usually hung on the wall.

Affluent Provençal households wanted their own versions of Paris style. These chairs, pictured at the upholsterer, are made in walnut. $1200-1600

One of a matching set of fruitwood chairs; the skilled and vivacious turning transforms a simple theme. $240-400

Provençal commodes are mainly either of three drawers with short legs or two drawers with longer, narrower legs. Handles are usually in leaf, or, as here, in shell-like form. *Courtesy of Gloucester House Antiques.* $11,200-14,400

Shaped tops with convex and concave drawer undulations typify Provençal commodes. 39" x 34" x 15". *Courtesy of Gloucester House Antiques.* $8000-9600

Below it is traditionally placed the pétrin, a trough shaped chest with a hinged top and sculpted legs. Its role in life is to store kneaded bread while it rises.

Look out, too, for the tamisadou, a small double-door cabinet originally used to refine flour and fitted with a mill inside and a handle on the outside. Today, most have lost their mechanics and are used simply as buffets.

This elegant eighteenth century walnut commode illustrates the two-drawer design on finer legs. 38" x 33" x 22".
Courtesy of Gloucester House Antiques.
$11,200-14,400

A walnut buffet à deux corps with elaborately shaped panels in the Avignon style.
Courtesy of Gloucester House Antiques.
$7200-8800

The Provençal obviously could not resist coming up with fresh designs, particularly for the kitchen, because they also devised the salière for storing salt and the farinière for flour. Small étagères were also popular and include not only the vaisselier, but also the verrier for glasses, the estagnié for pewter and the coutelière for knives - all self-contained units with bordered shelf fronts, sometimes with backs, sometimes without.

Commodes also received the distinctive Provençal touch as their fronts were made to undulate in convex and concave directions, all richly executed with carving almost baroque in feel, a style the French call *tourmenté*, in English, tormented.

You cannot leave Provence without also admiring the radassié, a distinctive rush seated banquette built like three or four chairs side by side, with arms at either end. Placed near the fireplace it was occasionally painted in olive green or gray blue and decorated with flowers and covered cushions.

Left: Simpler styles were favored in the mountainous hinterlands of Provence. This cherry armoire has little ornamentation apart from its escutcheons. *Courtesy of Gloucester House Antiques.* $4000-5600

A two-door one-drawer cupboard in cherry. The region boasts more exotic woods than most other parts of France, with almond, lemon and boxwood added to the repertoire. *Courtesy of Gloucester House Antiques.* $3200-4800

Lyons, Dauphiné and Savoy

The Saône and Rhône rivers meet majestically at Lyons as they flow on their ways to the Mediterranean, and they have brought wealth and vitality to the region over the centuries.

As one of France's gastronomic centers, Lyons should boast as many food related pieces as Provence, but with the exception of the garde-manger and pétrin, the range is less diverse.

Instead, the artisans' enthusiasms were often directed to small tables in various forms, including bedside tables, work tables, games tables and reading tables.

A distinct Italian influence can be seen, especially in the very decorative two drawer commodes of the region. Walnut is the most popular wood.

A speciality of the dauphinois region worth noting is the black varnish used to accentuate moldings and other key lines of a piece.

A mid-eighteenth century decorated armoire from the Dauphiné. A Louis XV style black lacquer writing desk from Lyons in contrasting city style. Courtesy of L'Encoignure, London. Armoire $6400-8000

The primitive shapes found in early pieces from the Savoy are evident in the lower half of this baby dresser in pine. *Courtesy of Gloucester House Antiques.* $4000-5600

There is often a touch of Italian influence in the well made walnut pieces from Lyons. This no drawers buffet is distinguished by a decorative ribbon motif above the doors and a classical urn and column carving between. *Courtesy of Gloucester House Antiques.* $4800-6400

The heavy rustic styling of furniture from the Haute Savoy is in strong contrast to the ornamentation of Lyons. This cupboard in mountain pine was originally painted blue. *Courtesy of Gloucester House Antiques.* $3200-4800

Made in one piece and with a cavity at the back for plates, this pine dresser is also from the Haute Savoy. *Courtesy of Gloucester House Antiques.* $4000-5600

Right: This eighteenth century pine armoire from the mountains was almost certainly made to be painted to suit local tastes. *Courtesy of Gloucester House Antiques.* $4000-5600

There are often similarities in feel between the simple outlines of furniture from the Savoy and those from Brittany. This pine cabinet is notable for the drawer between the two doors. *Courtesy of Gloucester House Antiques.* $4000-5600

Tables for needlework, reading and games were among the most popular of a wide range of table types emanating from the Dauphiné. This beautifully finished example is in walnut. *Courtesy of Gloucester House Antiques.* $2400-4000

Left: A finely-proportioned cherry table from north of Lyons. *Courtesy of Gloucester House Antiques.* $1600-4000

Burgundy, Bresse and Franche-Comté

Driving through Burgundy is like a high speed journey over a fine wine list as the names of world-renowned wines like Clos de Vougeot and Richebourg flash by one after the other.

This is a region which can, in a good year, be fertile and prosperous. But its people are hard working, sober and traditional in their ways.

This dichotomy is echoed by the regional shadings of furniture design. To the North the lines are more architectural and geometrical patterns are often favoured for decoration, while to the South some marquetry and the use of contrasting woods are evidence of a more vibrant approach.

The armoire is sometimes called a cabinet in Burgundy, and often has bun feet. In Bresse, a similar format using three panels

An armoire notable for its distinctive burr wood panels in the Southern Burgundy style, and a three-drawer fruitwood commode. Courtesy of L'Encoignure, London.

Left: A fruitwood armoire with a drawer in the base combines a square outline with the softening touches of partly turned panels and restrained carving. $2400-3600

The pivoting table was widely made in Burgundy, the Mâconnais and, especially, in the Châtillonais. The lyre shape was favored for the pivoting section of the base. It is sometimes called a vendange table due to is widespread use for outdoor meals during the grape harvest. $1200-2400

Below: The lively graining of this cherry buffet gives it vivacity without the need for elaborate carving. From the Yonne district. *Courtesy of Gloucester House Antiques.* $4800-5600

This was a pioneering space saving unit - when not in use it could be placed out of the way against a wall. The top of the table is in poplar, the base in burr elm. Early nineteenth century.

per door was utilized, but the feet are more often delicately curved. Here, too, contrasting door panel woods, such as walnut and burr ash, were favoured.

Buffets are often tall, and sometimes in Burgundy have a clock positioned under the cornice.

Since they eat so well in this region it should come as no surprise that the buffet vaisselier is more popular than the armoire. In Bresse they are even more numerous then armoires, as highly regarded and often more carefully made. Countless variations can be discovered, but perhaps the most notable example comprises a three door base with three drawers above. The panels of the doors

Rich, deep walnut is lifted by a simple but effective urn, bloom and tendril motif. $2400-3600

Another pivoting table, this time in cherry. This style took over from large, rectangular shaped tables in rural areas as the numbers of farm workers diminished and sizeable communal meals became less frequent. *Courtesy of Gloucester House Antiques.*

A small side table in pear. Fruitwood was the most popular choice in the region as a whole, followed by oak. 33" x 28". *Courtesy of Palmer Antiques.* $1600-3200

101

are in burr ash while the frame of the dresser is walnut. The top consists of four or five shelves over two small cupboards, one on each side, which were usually reserved for wines and liqueurs. This is the area in which to search out a fine and distinctive dresser.

This is also clock country, for every Bressan home boasts an horloge, usually in the violin shape of Louis XV. Decoration takes the form of undulating moldings, matching closely the local style for armoires, buffets and vaisseliers.

Elliptical medallions on the door traverses were used in Burgundy as well as Normandy, but in a slightly less ornamental style. This decorative armoire is in pear. *Courtesy of Palmer Antiques.* $6400-8000

A cherry buffet à un corps with a burr ash panel on the single door. *Courtesy of Gloucester House Antiques.* $1600-2400

Plenty of room at this substantial oak table for an extra guest. The drawers are for knives and forks and the table may well have come from a convent. *Courtesy of Gloucester House Antiques.* $8000-11,200

Left: A walnut single buffet, this time without a drawer. *Courtesy of Gloucester House Antiques.* $4800-6400

Right: A rare small two-door buffet in walnut with no faux-dormant. Single buffets are scarce in the Côte d'Or and the Dijonnais but numerous along the borders of Burgundy and Champagne. *Courtesy of Gloucester House Antiques.* $4000-5600

Examples from Bresse like this one in walnut and burr ash are also few and far between. Note the unusual design of the central panel. *Courtesy of Gloucester House Antiques.* $4800-6400

Small chests of drawers or commodes can be found in Bresse. They are usually quite sober in style with visual interest supplied by the shaped moldings and metalwork. This example is in ash, the most popular wood here after fruitwood and oak. *Courtesy of Gloucester House Antiques.* $4000-5000

A three-door walnut buffet or enfilade typifies the classic sober style of the northern part of the region. The north tended to reflect the influences of the Ile-de-France, Lorraine and the Flamand while the south was more Latin. *Courtesy of Gloucester House Antiques.* $4800-6400

Left: Chairs in a rich cherry with rush seats. *Courtesy of Gloucester House Antiques.* $800-1200 each.

The bun feet, rectangular lines and triple-panelled doors declare this to be a typical armoire of the Franche-Comté, although the style can also be found in Burgundy. Made in fruitwood it combines the influences of Louis XIII and Louis XIV. *Courtesy of Gloucester House Antiques.* $4800-5600

This rush-seated armchair in cherry is in the style known as 'bonne femme'. *Courtesy of Gloucester House Antiques.* $1200-1600

Left: Identifying the maker of a piece is a rare and special occasion, but this walnut armoire, found in England, displays several highly distinctive characteristics that declare it to be the work of Claude Laborier, one of the few recognised French provincial artisans of the nineteenth century. Laborier worked around Sennecy-le-Grand, towards the south-east of the region, just north of Mâcon. He specialized in making a particular style of armoire, large in dimensions, with steel hinges the length of each door and a drawer at the bottom. Examples of his work can be found in an excellent book on the region's furniture by Suzanne Tardieu-Dumont, based on the records of the Archives du Musée National des Arts et Traditions Populaires. $8000-9600

Laborier often worked, as here, in walnut. The cornice was straight, the doors combined three panels and the central section was a fluted faux-dormant.

Laborier's decoration combined the classicism of Mâcon with the floral art of Bresse.

The same species of wood was usually employed throughout but a different tone, like the burr walnut here, was used for the door panels.

A central keyhole flanked by two delicately formed steel handles was set into the drawer above a shell and flower motif.

The metalwork is among the most attractive to be found anywhere, and the keyhole decorations sometimes had extra side pieces extending towards the moldings.

Handsome hinges run the entire length of each door.

Some satisfying additional identification for the furniture detective. Hidden inside the armoire is a rail transport label which shows that on a date unknown it was transported to Nice Ville from Mâcon.

Louis XV influenced yet soberly decorated, this walnut Burgundian armoire has a drawer in the base which indicates that it comes from the south of the region. *Courtesy of Gloucester House Antiques.* $6400-8000

A rare single-door armoire, probably from the Franche-Comté. *Courtesy of Gloucester House Antiques.* $4800-5600

Below: A simple cherry armoire from the southern part of the region, where the profusion of armoires was caused by the impracticality of building integral cupboards in the local wood framed houses, as in Normandy. *Courtesy of Gloucester House Antiques.* $5600-7200

A selection of mainly southern pottery fills the shelves of a Comtois fruitwood armoire. *Courtesy of Gloucester House Antiques.* $4800-5600

Alsace and Lorraine

This picturesque region, close to the German border, can lay claim to being the birthplace of both Joan of Arc and Baron Haussmann, the man who conceived the wide boulevards of Paris.

Strasbourg, the capital of Alsace, is famed for its old half-timbered houses gathered around a rose colored cathedral built with Vosges sandstone, one of the greatest masterpieces of Gothic art.

But, once again, it is the influence of Louis XV which dominates the local furniture, albeit with an emphasis less on ornamentation than on mixed woods, interesting graining and burr finishes.

An instantly recognisable ingredient of Lorraine decoration is marquetry, which was used to highlight a range of motifs, such as stars, crosses, rosettes, swastikas and garlands. Moldings turned symmetrically on all four sides were also popular.

Armoires were favoured for the belle chambre or bedroom, normally made with two doors and two drawers, except in the Meuse, where there were no drawers. Ornamentation is sober and what little there is comes from the mixture of woods, marquetry and the frequent use of the long pointed star motif.

Buffets à deux corps were often made in a highly distinctive style, in which the two sections, upper and lower, resemble a single buffet placed on top of another of similar design.

Tables are mainly in oak and rectangular with H-shaped stretchers. Commodes are extremely rare.

An undeniable Renaissance feel can be recognised in some Alsatian pieces, alongside the combined influences of Switzerland, the Rhine and Italy.

Armoires have an architectural structure, with columns at either side and often in the center as well. Ornamentation includes cartouches, human masks and stylized foliage.

A vibrant mixture of fruitwood panelling and marquetry with an oak framework makes this small armoire a fine example of Lorraine craftsmanship. Unusually, the central traverse runs at an angle. $4800-5600

The Lorraine star sits at the center of well-made marquetry and inlay.

111

This cupboard is made in walnut with oak sides and two doors with a drawer between. 72" x 34". $4800-6400

A discreet marquetry star below the cornice helps identify this piece's Lorraine heritage.

Alsatian buffets à deux corps often look like a marriage of two low buffets. This example, in pitch pine, is a variation on the theme, with a fall front to the top section. 79" x 53" x 20". *Courtesy of Gloucester House Antiques.* $4800-6400

Characteristic Alsatian tables have turned legs with X-shaped stretchers or legs angled outwards with a four-square stretcher system.

The same diverging legs re-appear on the distinctive seats of the region. Square plain seats have highly decorative backs, perhaps featuring serpents or vases, over four legs which appear at first sight to be collapsing hopelessly in an outwards direction.

Three-drawer buffets with two doors and a decorative central panel were a popular design. This is in oak from Lorraine. 70" x 37" x 20". *Courtesy of Gloucester House Antiques.* $4000-5600

Ardennes and Champagne

In summer the sun steadily ripens the grapes that are used to make the region's famous Champagne marques. But the winter months can bring harsher weather, and the style of the furniture reflects this change in climate as you travel further North.

Furniture from the Ardennes and Champagne has a distinctly robust quality which is emphasised by the widespread use of oak in preference to walnut.

Narrow door panels were favored and these make for a feeling of considerable height in the larger pieces, while decoration was kept to a minimum, with straight lines preferred to curved and carving, when seen, normally in light relief.

Armoires were made in polished oak, and only occasionally in walnut. Well proportioned, they have double doors with a large drawer in the base and simple marquetry for decoration, often featuring a star or stars in the Lorraine manner.

Oak buffets with two doors, large central panels and three doors above are most often seen in Champagne, while the buffets à deux corps generally come in a sober Louis XV style, often with between three and five drawers set in the base between a pair of doors.

Vigorous moldings on the central traverses of this walnut armoire suggest it comes from the Bassigny. *Courtesy of Palmer Antiques.* $5600-7200

A classic Champagne area fruitwood buffet, its restrained ornamentation serves to stress the beauty of the wood and the sheer wholesomeness of the piece. *Courtesy of Palmer Antiques.* $4800-6400

Left: Curiously shaped legs and tiny drawer give this table a strong personality despite its small size. The legs are in oak and the skirting and top in fruitwood. 29" x 44" *Courtesy of Palmer Antiques.* $1600-2400

Robustness, simplicity and quality are the hallmarks of the region's best oak furniture. $4000-4800

The squareness of the overall shape and side panelling is softened by the shaped Louis XV influenced front panels. $4000-4800

Below: Lack of a drawer indicates that this is an early oak armoire from the Bassigny. $4000-4800

The dresser, called le ménager in this region, is a popular piece of furniture and comes in fruitwood in Champagne and oak in the Ardennes. The base contains three molded doors with three drawers above, each with a simple steel knob. Above it the rack has three shelves supported by turned balustrades and edged by a molded rim to retain the plates.

Commodes are scarcer than other types of furniture and are likely to be Louis XV or Louis XVI influenced. Beds were often painted in clear gray.

Like Provence, this region has some distinctive small-scale specialities. One is the bahut-laiterie, a single door buffet with moldings and a gallery of spindles to let the air in, and a single drawer above. It was used to store dairy products.

Others are the salignon, a small salt container looking like a flattened pyramid; the godelier, a rack of three or four shelves with notches to hold forks and spoons; and the porte-essuie, a small étagère to support a roller for napkins.

The severe lines and dark oak patina give this armoire an architectural feeling. Barely visible are faintly chiselled patterns at the very tops of the doors. *Courtesy of Gloucester House Antiques.* $5600-7200

A metamorphic chair. Provincial town houses would often have substantial built-in bookcases. $400-800

The design permits easy conversion into library steps.

A prettily decorated pendulum is the feature of this painted pine clock from the Southern Ardennes.

Picardy and Flanders

A taste for rich Gothic and Renaissance style ornamentation has long distinguished the architecture and furniture of France's north-eastern-most corner.

The proximity of neighbors Belgium and Germany can be sensed in much of the carving and decorative work, while even the names of pieces have a different look, such as the ribbank, a two-door cupboard, the spinder, a food cupboard, and the dresche, a type of buffet.

In fact, the ribbank is one of the pieces most commonly found in northern farms. It is a square cupboard on bun feet with heavy geometrical carving.

More elegant, perhaps, are the various low buffets found in the region. Double buffets are scarce but single buffets and those with dresser racks above are highly characteristic.

Some are so long that they boast eight doors, notably in Picardy, where they are often surmounted by dresser shelves and are known as traites. Their sizes depended on the capacity of the rooms for which they were

A three-drawer fruitwood commode made around 1775 in northern France. *Courtesy of L'Encoignure, London.* $4800-6400

intended, and the variations of shapes and sizes are therefore enormous. In Artois, though hardly ever in Picardy, you can find a version which features a series of shelves across the centre of the buffet base, and which is known as a séage.

In the region overall, they often call their various buffets and dressers bancs de ménage, a name which reflects their functional day to day housekeeping usage. Look out, too, for rare models with a section of grandfather clock built into them.

Armoires are sometimes known as presses, and were made mainly for bedrooms. Apart from molded panels there is very little decoration.

Farmhouse tables were long and often given heavily turned legs in the Renaissance style. Circular drop-leaf tables were also made in Flanders.

Preferred woods were pear and apple up to the seventeenth century, oak, elm and lime at the start of the eighteenth century, and thereafter, wild cherry, plum and cherry.

Here the speciality piece is the égouttoir, an open trough on four feet and sometimes with a shelf underneath. It is a combined draining board and decorative display unit intended for large kitchens.

A Picardy buffet in oak, recognizable by its three shaped central drawers. *Courtesy of Gloucester House Antiques.* $4800-6400

Near neighbor, the Flamand buffet has a curved front and four doors. This one in oak is eighteenth century and has a superb marble top. 63" x 37" x 24". *Courtesy of Gloucester House Antiques.* $6400-8000

Left: An oak buffet with a small central drawer. *Courtesy of Gloucester House Antiques.* $4800-6400

Clean lines elevate this narrow oak armoire. $4000-5600

A Picardy traite with four doors. This is half the length of some. *Courtesy of Gloucester House Antiques.* $6400-8000

Ile-de-France

The influence is urban but the execution is provincial. A charming walnut bureau of the early nineteenth century. 45" x 54" x 20". *Courtesy of Gloucester House Antiques.* $6400-8800

"The garden of Paris" is how the Ile-de-France is sometimes described, and if there was one region which could not escape the influence of the big city, this was it.

As an established supplier of food and goods to Paris over the centuries, the Ile-de-France relied on a close relationship which affected every facet of daily life.

The local artisans were profoundly influenced by the styles and techniques which their counterparts in nearby Paris were promoting, and the outcome was a general degree of perfection in construction, shape and finish which was remarkable by the standards of craftspeople in more isolated provinces.

Rustic shapes were largely abandoned, but, nevertheless, the country feel was not lost altogether.

In the more modest homes of the region there was still a demand for honest, strong furniture that could happily survive in an environment that was meant to be well lived in. Fancy veneers or delicate finishes were fine for the salons of Paris, but they would not have lasted long in the farmhouse of a large family.

In many respects, the furniture of the Ile-de-France is the hardest of all to distinguish. All types of furniture were made and in a range of fruit and forest woods. Louis XV influences predominated, but without the fanciful variations introduced elsewhere. Here, they skilfully reproduced many aspects of Paris work in terms of quality, but retained that touch of additional sturdiness that singles out a good country piece.

The use of apple wood brings an appealing lightness of color to this otherwise simple armoire. 86" x 54" x 30". *Courtesy of Palmer Antiques.* $5600-7200

By replacing the panels of this armoire's doors with wire mesh the linen and bedding stored inside can be attractively displayed. *Courtesy of Palmer Antiques.* $4800-6400

One of a set of six oak dining chairs, the high back and rich upholstery acknowledge the influences of nearby Paris. *Courtesy of Palmer Antiques.* $4000-8000 set

The use of cherry and the overall look declare this to be a provincial piece, but the classical columns at either side and the ormolu trimmings reveal the Paris connection. *Courtesy of Palmer Antiques.* $4800-5600

An eighteenth century walnut fauteuil. The region's craftsmen achieved a high degree of perfection in their work. *Courtesy of Gloucester House Antiques.* $800-1200

A painted pine display cabinet of the type often found in small chateaux. *Courtesy of Gloucester House Antiques.* $2400-3200

Left: A butcher's table with characteristic brass trimmings and marble top. Today these nineteenth century tables are highly versatile, looking equally at home in kitchen, bathroom and living room. *Courtesy of Gloucester House Antiques.* $4000-7200

Bakers' and butchers' tables are becoming increasingly scarce. They were made originally in a wide range of shapes, sizes and decorative finishes. Here, the frieze adds a gothic touch. *Courtesy of Gloucester House Antiques.* $4000-7200

Glossary

Construction

chantourné, turned on all sides
corniche (la), cornice
corniche droite, straight cornice
corniche cintré, arched cornice
décor cannelé (le), fluted decoration
encadrement (le, l'), frame
enroulé en coquille d'escargot, rolled in snail shell shape
entrée de serrure (la, l'), keyhole decoration
faux-dormant (le), false frame
galbé, curved (feet)
garnitures metalliques (les), metal decorations
gâteau (le), roundel
gond (le), hinge
loupe (la), burr
miche (la), bun foot
montants (les), uprights
monté sur sabots, sitting on shoe feet
mouluré, decorated with moldings
ossature (la, l'), framework or structure
panneaux (les), panels
pieds cambrés (les), arched feet
placage (la), veneering
poignée (la), handle

siège paillé (le), rush seating
tiroir (le), drawer
traverse basse découpée (la), carved base crosspiece
vantaux (les), armoire doors

Furniture

armoire (la, l'), tall cupboard or wardrobe
bancelle (la), trestle seat
berceau (le), cradle
buffet (le), sideboard
buffet à deux corps (le), double buffet
buffet à glissants (le), buffet with small upper tier
chaise (la), chair
commode (la), chest of drawers
coffre (le), chest
enfilade (la, l'), long buffet
encoignure (la, l'), corner cupboard
étagère (la, l'), shelves, often small shelved table
fauteuil (le), armchair
garde-manger (le), food cupboard
pétrin (le), dough trough
siège (le), seat
table (la), table

vasselier (le), dresser

Wood

amandier (le, l'), almond
bouleau (le), birch
cerisier (le), cherry
châtaignier (le), chestnut
chêne (le), oak
citronnier (le), lemon
cormier (le), service
frêne (le), ash
hêtre (le), beech
mélèze (le), larch
merisier (le), wild cherry
murier (le), mulberry
noyer (le), walnut
orme (le, l'), elm
ormeau (le, l'), young elm
peuplier (le), poplar
pin (le), pine
poirier (le), pear
pommier (le), apple
prunier (le), plum
saule (le), willow
tilleul (le), lime

Bibliography

Gauthier, J. Stany, *La Connaissance des Meubles Régionaux Français*, Paris, France; Editions d'Art Charles Moreau, 1996.

Tardieu-Dumont, Suzanne. *Bourgogne, Bresse, Franche-Comté*. Paris, France; Berger-Levrault, 1981.

Also in the same series from the Archives du Musée National Des Arts Et Des Traditions Populaires: *Normandie, Lyonnais, Savoie-Dauphiné, Nord-Picardie, Provence*.

Index

almond, 126
amboyna, 23
Angers, Loire Valley, 63
Anjou, Loire Valley, 63
apple, 26, 126
Arles, Provence, 87, 91
armoire, name derivation, 16
armoirette, 43
artisans, travelling, 14, 29, 30
Artois, 119
ash, 26, 126
Avignon, Provence, 87
Avranches, Normandy, 42

bacheratéguy, 79
bahut-laiterie, 116
banc de ménage, 119
Bassigny, Ardennes, 114, 115
Beaucaire, Provence, 87, 91
Beaune, Burgundy, 24
beech, 26, 126
birch, 26, 126
Boulle, André-Charles, 19
Breton, Lower, style, 56
Breton, Upper, style, 56
buffet à glissants, 91
buffet de chasse, Angoumois, 74
buffet Nantais, 71, 75
burr ash, 23
burr elm, 23

Caen, Normandy, 38, 48
Calvados, Normandy, 46
canapé, 88

Cantal, Auvergne, 85
Cauchoise armoire, 48
chantourné, 67
châpeau de gendarme cornice, 8, 40, 48, 56, 57, 68
Charente, Poitou, 64
Charles X, 22
Châtillon, Burgundy, 100
Cherbourg, Normandy, 47
cherry, 23, 26, 27, 126
chestnut, 26, 126
Clessé, Saône-et-Loire, 36
Colbert, 19
Comtat, Provence, 91
Cornouaille, Brittany, 60
coutelière, 94
craftsmen, local, 30

demi-chantourné, 67
Directoire period, 21
Dômes, Auvergne, 85
dresche, 118

égouttoir, 119
elm, 26, 27, 126
Empire period, 21
encoignure, 91
enfilade, 71, 75
escargot feet, 9, 13
estagnié, 94
Eure, Normandy, 43

faux-dormant, 32, 39
Fécamp, Normandy, 38
Finistère, Brittany, 56
Flers, Normandy, 47
Fontenay, Vendée, 69
Fourques, Provence, 89

Gobelin project, 19
godelier, 116
gothic, 16, 118
Guérande, Brittany, 56

homme debout, 70

Ile-de-Noirmoutier, Vendée, 71
Ile-et-Vilaine, Brittany, 57

jardinière, armoire, 48

joints, tenon and mortice, 31

kingwood, 23

Laborier, Claude, 31, 106, 107, 108
Labourd, Basque, 79
larch, 26, 126
Lebrun, Charles, 19
lemon, 26, 126
Léon, Brittany, 60
lime, 26, 126
Louis Philippe, 11, 22
Louis XIII, 19
Louis XIV, 13, 19
Louis XV, 11, 18, 19
Louis XVI, 20
lovebirds, motif, 40, 45, 50, 87
Lower Navarre, Basque, 79
Luçon, Vendée, 69

Mâcon, Burgundy, 106, 107
mahogany, 23, 26, 38, 77
Maine, Loire Valley, 61
manjadou, 91
Marais, Vendée, 69
Marigny, Marquis de, 20
medallions, elliptical, 40, 102
Meissonier, 19
ménager, 116
metalwork, 32, 33, 67, 69
Meuse, Lorraine, 111
Middle Ages, 16
mixte, 67
Morbihan, Brittany, 56, 57
mulberry, 26, 126

Nantes, Brittany, 26, 59
Nantes, Vendée, 68
Narbonne, Languedoc, 82
Nîmes, Languedoc, 82, 83

oak, 19, 26, 27, 126
Orléans, Loire Valley, 61

palier, 53
panetière, 82, 91
Pays D'Auge, Normandy, 48
pear, 26, 126
pegs, 31
pelican, motif, 48, 52

Percier and Fontaine, 21
Perpignan, Roussillon, 82
pétrin, 36, 89, 93
pine, 26, 43, 126
Pineau, 19
poplar, 26, 126
porte-essuie, 116

radassié, 88, 94
Renaissance, 19
Rennes, Brittany, 8, 56, 57, 58
Restoration period, 22
ribbank, 118
rococo, 19
Rouen, Normandy, 38, 48

Saint-Nicolas D'Aliermont, Normandy, 42
Saint-Rémy, Provence, 91
salignon, 116
Sennecy-le-Grand, Burgundy, 30, 106
séage, 119
service, 26, 126
Soule, Basque, 79
spiders, 26
spinder, 118

table à glissants, 37
tables, extending, 41
tamisadou, 93
Tarascon, Provence, 87
Toulon, Provence, 87
Toulouse, Languedoc, 8, 83
Touraine, Loire Valley, 61
tourmenté, style, 94
Tours, Loire Valley, 63
traite, 120
transitional period, 20

Velay, Auvergne, 85, 86
vendange, table, 100, 101
verrier, 94

wedding armoire, 30, 50
wild cherry, 23, 26, 126
woods, mixing, 25, 26, 27
woodworm, 33

Yonne, Burgundy, 100
Yvetot, Normandy, 38